If Only Reacl

MW01231875

Adoption Stories From the Heart of the Touched

New Beginnings International
Children's & Family Services

Compiled by:
Tom Velie and New Beginnings

Edited and Compiled by: Shelle Castles-Melton

Cover Design by: Michele Shubert

If Only The Hands That Reach Could Touch
Adoption Stories From the Heart of the Touched

Tom Velie, New Beginnings and Shelle Castles-Melton

Printed in the United States by Morris Publishing
3212 East Highway 30
Kearney, NE 68847
1-800-650-7888

All scriptural quotes are from the *New King James Version* of the Bible.

Printed in the United States of America

ISBN 0-9767529-0-5

To Debbie - my "partner" in this great endeavor of ministry and life.

To Cori & Shaina - my beautiful daughters who have blessed our lives and opened the door to adoption for our family. Your mom and I love you!

To Shelle – thank you for your willingness to sacrifice your time and expertise so others could be "touched." You and Scott are special.

To those who wrote the stories, and who "are" the stories – this is for YOU!

TO ORDER ADDITIONAL COPIES OF THIS BOOK:

All profits from the sale of this book are donated to New Beginnings to promote the adoption of children into "forever" families.

New Beginnings International Children's & Family Services
P.O. Box 7055
Tupelo, MS 38802
662-842-6752
info@newbeginnings.us

Or, order online at:

www.newbeginnings.us

Tom Velie may be contacted at:

P. O. Box 7055
Tupelo, MS 38802
tom@newbeginnings.us

Legacy of an adopted child

Once there were two women
Who never knew each other

One you do not remember
The other you call mother

Two different lives
Shaped to make yours one

One became your guiding star
The other became your sun

The first gave you life
And the second taught you to live it

The first gave you a need for love
And the second was there to give it

One gave you a nationality
The other gave you a name

One gave you the seed of talent
The other gave you an aim

One gave you emotions
The other calmed your fears

One saw your first sweet smile
The other dried your tears

One gave you up
It was all that she could do

The other prayed for a child
And God led her straight to you

And now you ask me
Through your tears

The ago old questions
Through the years

Heredity or environment
Which are you a product of?

Neither my darling, neither
Just two different kinds of love.

- Anonymous

INTRODUCTION
Jack E. Yonts, Sr.

A highway billboard made a brief but bold statement, it simply said, "Forty million babies will not pay social security." This tragic statement tells only part of the story of the multiplied millions of infant lives who were not allowed to come to birth.

Abortion has become the scourge of America and much of the world.

New Beginning was born as a righteous alternative for young women, mostly teenagers, who find themselves with unplanned pregnancies. Behind the scenes of this magnificent institution is the story of an intense burden, selfless sacrifice and empathetic love, which emanates from the staff of those at New Beginnings.

The story of this successful endeavor is both enlightening and moving, you will appreciate these acts of charity personified. Many childless couples have been blessed by the arrival of a beautiful, tiny infant whom the birthmother chose not to abort, all because of New Beginnings. I personally have been blessed by two beautiful and loving granddaughters because of New Beginnings. You will not soon forget this story of Divine love in action.

We are all adopted – into God's Family…

This book is dedicated to the memory of Grover Nolan Burns (1907-1994) and William Alvin Velie (1900-1993). Without them I would not exist. They are my grandfathers and they continue to live - because I live.

Grover and William (Bill) were quiet, hard-working men who valued their relationship with God and their families above all else.

Grover was born in the hills of northern Wisconsin and knew everything there was to know about farming, walking to school in the snow, playing basketball in the days when 30 points was a high-scoring game and, most importantly, being a "Grandpa."

When I was 16 and feeling the call to the ministry, my Pastor asked me to meet him in church at 7:00 a.m. on a Saturday morning. Visions of visiting the hospital, where sick would be raised from their deathbeds, danced through my head as the great day of my entry into the ministry approached.

Standing in the church foyer to greet us was Grandpa Burns -the Church janitor (his retirement job). Pastor Tandberg then introduced me to my new ministry. And…for the next few years I ministered alongside Mr. Clean, Ajax, Grandpa Burns and a host of other cleaning and painting supplies. But I wouldn't trade that experience, and what I learned during those years, for anything on this earth.

Grandpa Velie's hometown doesn't exist anymore, but my Dad walked with me along the old train tracks several years ago to

2

talk about the old family. Grandpa Velie grew up on a houseboat with his preacher father as they traveled up and down the Mississippi River preaching the gospel.

I have a picture of Grandpa Velie standing in front of a huge sign on the side of the houseboat that simply reads *4JesusRU*.

He took my brother and me fishing and camping. We marveled as he killed a monstrous, life-threatening, and slithering garden snake.

And oh what treasures the little shop in his basement held! Grinders, tool and die sets, tackle boxes and the list goes on. What a place for a grandson and a grandfather to share. They weren't wealthy and they weren't well-known.

Grandpa Burns and Grandpa Velie both made tires. Grandpa Burns sweated for over 40 years in the curing room and Grandpa Velie served for over 40 years as a machinist.

They never complained about the hard work, they never missed a day of work and they paid their bills.

They both endured the Depression and so, even in retirement, they continued to save money while living on their small pensions and Social Security checks.

However, Grandpa Burns always had mints in his pocket and Grandpa Velie provided us with Black Jack gum. In our young eyes – these were rich grandpas!

I was born to Eunice Burns and William Thomas Velie and life was grand.

In fact, until my wife, Debbie, and I adopted our two daughters, Cori and Shaina, earthly adoption was not a part of the Burns or Velie families. So, you may ask, why have we chosen to work with troubled children, struggling birthmothers, crying babies and anxious adoptive parents for the past twenty years? The answer is simple…

Because every child deserves to experience what I experienced because of my two grandpas. I was loved unconditionally. I never went to bed hungry. I was never abused—in any way. I was never afraid in my own home. I wore clean and decent clothes. I was raised to respect the Pastor, the Sunday school teachers, the public school teachers, the neighbors, the disabled, the simple, the elders, my parents, and everyone else in life. I was raised to know that faithful meant faithful and loyal meant loyal—to your children, to your wife, to your job and to the Lord.

On the day one of my Grandpas died, he informed his family that it was payday. Thinking that he meant it was the day his Social Security check arrived, the family replied, "Yes Daddy, your check comes today."

When Grandpa said, "No, I mean today IS payday. . . " they understood. Grandpa knew who he worked for and he loved his Master.

My grandpas taught me that adoption was about being a part of God's family. And so…when my Payday comes, I pray that I will stand between these gentle giants once again, knowing that my work resulted in happier lives for a few of God's favorite children…"the adopted."

I'm thankful to be one of them…

4

Adoption is NOT a Label
Tom Velie

Returning home one day from a board meeting at the University in Oxford with my friend, Thad, who was sitting in the passenger seat, my cell phone rang. When the friend on the phone asked who was with me, I unconsciously replied, "Thad, my black friend from my social work class." I was simply describing who Thad was – or so I thought.

After hanging up the phone, Thad, with his ever-calm nature, asked, "Why did you use my color to describe me? You could have easily said, 'He's my friend from the social work class.'"

He was right: we were the only two guys in the social work class.

Labels - we all tend to use them. And, so it is with the labels of ADOPTION, ADOPTED, ADOPTEES and ADOPTED CHILD.

I cringe when I read sensational headline titles such as, ***Adopted Child*** *Kills Store Clerk in Drug-Induced Rampage.*

Why not put the title, ***Birth Child*** *Kills Store Clerk in Drug-Induced Rampage* in similar headlines?

Our prisons are full of "fatherless" adults, our foster homes are overflowing with children who were removed from "birthparent" homes, and "birth children" share a majority of the same challenges that are faced by "adopted children."

Adoption doesn't define a child's hair color, skin color, IQ, artistic ability, height, shoe size or much of anything else.

5

Research shows us that, except for children born to their biological parents who remain living in intact two-parent families, the outcome for children who join their families through adoption, and who remain in two-parent homes, are better than for any other group. In other words, adoption is more often than not - predictive of a successful life.

Thad is my "friend," Cori and Shania are my "daughters," and Ben is an "adult community leader" who joined his family through adoption. They're all normal, healthy, happy human beings and the labels of color and adoption just don't fit into the description of who they are. Those labels do not define them.

As you read through the variety of stories in this book, please notice how adoption is an "event" that occurred at some point in time and not an identifier that surrounds itself in every adopted persons life.

Children are reaching out and adoption is the bridge to "touch" a family.

Enjoy the stories that are written by everyday people in everyday language. We've edited the stories only for ease of reading, because we want you to know that families who have adopted, children who have joined families through adoption - and all the rest of us involved in the adoption process, from attorneys to ministers, to nurses, to doctors and to social workers, are just everyday folks.

Across America, and across the oceans, the hands of children are reaching out. They need homes. They need moms and dads. They need grandparents. And they need someone to touch. Perhaps they need you. . .

Truths About Adoption

Adoption terminates the rights and responsibilities of the biological parents and transfers them to the adoptive family so the child can become a full and permanent member of the adoptive family.

Adoption is time-honored social institution that helps children who need a family find one.

Adoption is a good choice for teens and women experiencing a crisis pregnancy.

Adoption is a good choice for children.

Options counseling and adoption counseling must take into account the individual needs of each client depending on her social, emotional, cognitive and spiritual needs as well as her physical needs and resources.

Adoption information as well as information on her other options must be presented to every woman involved with a crisis pregnancy to assure that she has the information she needs to make a fully informed choice.

The best environment for a person to experience healthy development is a permanent, secure two-parent family.

Parenting is a choice and a commitment to provide a stable, loving, and permanent environment for a child.

The decision to not be a parent, when accompanied by an adoption plan, is not abandonment.

Adoption is a life transition that can be difficult and emotional; it is not a lifelong grieving and recovery process.

Formal adoption provides security and legal protection for a child that cannot be matched by guardianship or other informal care processes.

There is no substitute for a permanent, loving Christian family.

Adoption-Parenting counseling can be a process by which the ordinary can be transformed into the extraordinary. It is a way to reframe the problem that requires adequate preparation, finding the place of most potential and believing there is more than one right answer.

Extraordinary Birthmothers
Debbie Velie

I'm writing this as I sit in the hospital with one of our birthmothers.

She has chosen adoption because she believes she is making the best choice for her baby - and for herself.

She chose and has met the adoptive couple.

This extraordinary birthmother is an awesome person – strong, intelligent and caring. She is willing to bear the grief of her decision because she believes it is the right thing to do. She has been blessed by the joy the adoptive parents are experiencing.

Adoption is my life. It's my work. It's my ministry - and it has blessed my life on a personal level.

Twenty-three years ago, my life was forever changed when they placed our daughter, Cori, in my arms.

Three years later, our baby girl, Shaina, blessed our family. I cannot imagine my life without my girls. I know I could not love them more if they had been born to me.

I believe in adoption because I have seen the blessing it has been in the lives of birthmothers, adoptive couples and many precious children.

Sadly, adoption is often misunderstood. Critics believe birthmothers choose adoption because they "don't want" the baby, when exactly the opposite is true. Birthmothers choose

9

adoption because they are loving and unselfish. They put the well being of the baby above their own feelings and emotions. They believe that the best plan for their baby is to be raised in a two-parent family that is emotionally, spiritually and financially stable.

Our birthmothers are a diverse group – I've worked with clients as young as 12 and as old as 44. They come from all economic backgrounds and their circumstances are all unique to them – but they all have one thing in common. . . They do not believe they are prepared to parent the child they are expecting.

I admire and respect these young women and their willingness to take this less traveled road because they believe, for them; it is the right thing to do.

These birthmothers are reassured by what the adoptive couples must go through to be approved. They are comforted by the fact that they can get pictures and updates about the baby after placement. They are glad to hear from me when I have done birthparent search counseling with adults who were adopted as babies, that their precious adopted baby is thankful for the decision their birthmother made. Adopted children are not angry at their birthmother. They acknowledge that their birthmothers' decision must have been very difficult and emotional, but they wish to contact her to say thank you for blessing me with a wonderful home and a great life.

I'm thankful that adoption allowed me to be a mother to two wonderful daughters and I'm blessed to have adoption be my life's work.

Everyday Kids
Anonymous

Today, my oldest son, who is two-and-a-half-years-old, announced, "I need a motorcycle!" He wanted to drive his grandma to see the buffalo that live on a farm not too far from our house.

As a mother who desires to protect my children from harm, potential or otherwise, the first thing that came to mind was, *"What?! There is no way you are getting a motorcycle! Do you know how dangerous they are and how many people get killed or injured while riding them? You're only two and what would have put that into your head?"*

But looking into my son's sincere, glittering brown eyes and serious face, I chose instead, to smile and realize that this was an opportunity to build fellowship with him.

His dreams and desires came from a pure, albeit naïve, heart. He didn't understand the dangers involved; he just believed that a motorcycle would be a good way to show grandma the countryside.

There is no doubt my two-year-old needs guidance and training, but I'm learning to allow room for dreams and creativity.

I know that if I project my fears and worries on my little child too soon, I am robbing him of something incredibly precious.

And more than anything, I desire to bind strings of fellowship and trust with my children so they know I am someone they can

11

trust not only to provide for their needs, but that I am trustworthy with their feelings and dreams.

My youngest son, who just turned one, is discovering the joys of mobility. I suspect, although he hasn't asked for a motorcycle - mostly due to limited speech - he certainly wouldn't be opposed to the idea. He loves to chase after his older brother and be involved in everything and anything he does.

They are quite a pair. Their personalities are extremely unique, but complement each other so well. It is obvious to me that God is doing an awesome work by bringing our family together in the way He has planned for us.

Both of my sons joined our family through adoption at an early age. They haven't reached an age where they can understand what adoption means in their little lives, but I know a day is coming when they will need to reconcile that reality.

Their adoption is only one part of a big complicated world they will have to work through as they grow older. I'm looking forward to being a part of that process.

In many ways, our family is very similar to that of one that has only biological children and in other ways it is very unique.

Our boys do not share our ethnic background and therefore do not look like us, but I have to admit I do not even notice until someone points it out. Maybe that's just a mom's special measure of grace; I've never met a mother who didn't think their child wasn't the most beautiful, gifted, intelligent child in the world.

I was not able to be a part of the experience of birthing my children but I am privileged to have the experience of raising the children God gives me. To miss the little opportunities to build a healthy relationship with them is just unthinkable. So does that mean there is a motorcycle in my boys' futures? Well, thankfully they are still young so we have some time to hash out the details before it becomes a real concern for this mom.

However, my husband doesn't really see why I should be so worried – at least my oldest son knows that you wear a helmet when you go riding. Apparently it's a guy thing.

Never A Dull Moment
Suzan Hudspeth

Our adopted son was a surprise from the start. Because of unique circumstances involving the birthmother's preferences, the waiting time was shorter than expected. Even though it caught us off guard – we were thrilled!

That was six years ago and I've always had a story to tell about him. And along with all the laughter, he has helped me learn several important lessons:

Goal setting: Set goals – not age limits. Take potty training for example. I always said that I would never have a child who was not potty trained by two years of age. My son barely qualified at three and a half! During this trying time, I learned two important things; you cannot make a child GO to the bathroom and, more importantly, my son's smart, funny, healthy and happy. So, what's the big deal with having a three-year-old that's not potty trained?

False prophecy: Be careful when you say "never." For example, "I will never allow my child to get in trouble at school without major consequences at home." Every expectant parent makes these, "I would never let my child do…" statements. This one was made before a highly energetic, extremely active, somewhat mischievous "Dennis the Menace" arrived in our lives. If I had stuck to this statement, he would be forever banished to his room. Since becoming a parent, I have recanted many of my "never" statements.

I also realized that there are worse things than swinging your arms in line, playing with your neighbor's feet at nap time and changing seats during lunch. In other words, let the punishment fit the offense. Also, a flat-out pardon is often in order.

Being friendly: To have friends, be friendly. My son never meets a stranger. In restaurants, airports, hotels, stores and at school, he always find someone to talk to - this could be part of the school trouble that I told you about. He visits with the principal, the waitress, the greeter at the store – anyone who will stop and listen. Who would have thought that such a small child would be able to help me be friendlier? But I have found myself making polite conversation with complete strangers much more often than I did before he came along.

Children are a gift from God and each one is special in a different way. I have two children who entered our family through adoption. My daughter is completely different from my son. There are no precise rules to follow when parenting and who would want it any other way? God made us unique! That's what makes life unpredictable, fun and exciting.

God's Timing
Barron D. Price

Acts 15:18
Known unto God are all his works from the beginning of the world.

God's providence and the beauty of His excellence are beyond the meager efforts of mankind to fathom. While we struggle to find our place and way in life, He has a plan that is perfect and glorious. When we recognize the depth of His love, not only for us, but also for the whole world, it is easy to place our complete trust in Him.

Three years into our marriage, God allowed us the thrill of expectancy as we learned that we were with child. Due to complications, our son was born prematurely, but God allowed him to develop healthily.

Two years later, we were blessed with another son, but after stern warnings from the physicians, and much consternation from my wife, who desperately wanted a daughter, it was determined that this should be the extent of our family.

As year was added to year, the longing for a daughter intensified. Every time my wife learned of an unwanted pregnancy her anticipation would intensify that this could be her opportunity to obtain her great desire to adopt, and raise a daughter. Time after time our hopes were dashed.

After years of disappointment and a reservation to God's will, something miraculous happened.

16

We contacted New Beginnings and miraculously, only two weeks later we were made aware of an opportunity that sounded too good to be true. In God's time, He provided exactly what we had so longed for.

The circumstances surrounding our opportunity may appear to some as coincidence. Others may view them as punishment or judgment, but God in His mercy, glory, and majesty has a wonderful way of working all things together for good to them who love the Lord and are the called according to His purpose.

When we could not understand, God was fully aware when the time was right. He knew all the time. And when we needed those loving arms of a daughter, and loving hands to hold and guide, God provided them through the unfortunate circumstances of another.

Words could never express the joys this loving birthmother gave to a family, a church, a community and scores of individuals because she chose life.

We anticipate the time when she too can receive the embrace from the arms of this daughter who is so grateful to have been chosen into our family.

Our daughter has known from her earliest days of the miracle she was to us. She proudly proclaims that she has two mothers.

For her senior paper, she chose to write on the subject of abortion. She realizes that she could have easily been cheated out of her opportunity to live. She took advantage of this opportunity to expose the hideousness of many of the procedures in hopes that she might inspire others to always choose life - so that loving arms can continue to reach, and loving hands can touch and share God's love.

Everything Has Its Place
Suzan Hudspeth

I always knew that my four-year-old son was particular with his things and that he liked his colors and blocks sorted and neat. How obsessive this behavior was never impacted me until we went grocery shopping one day.

It was an everyday trip to the store with my son and daughter. It had become a habit for them each to get something from the candy aisle when we got ready to go through the checkout line. This process often took quite some time with so many varieties of candy to choose from.

On this particular day, I was in a hurry and had told them, "No candy today." As I was checking out, I noticed that my son over in the next aisle where the candy was. I kept calling him, telling him to come on – we were not buying any candy. He just stood there – trying to choose his candy, or so I thought.
By the time I went to get him, I had become quite irritated.

As I approached him, he said, "Just a minute, Mom. I'm not finished yet." There he was, in the grocery store, straightening up the candy display. Every M & M, Lifesaver, Bubblegum and Tic-Tac were all back in their rightful place, sorted by color and variety.

Today, at six, he can run the weed eater, stack wood, clean his room (much better than his older sister) and he knows where most of his toys are. I'm sure that at some point "messy" therapy might be needed.

But for now, this mom's glad *everything has its place*!

Riff Raff
Andreas Kjernald

The ancient pagan world didn't consider infant children as persons. Actually, it was the father who had to acknowledge that the child was his, so that the child could be received into the family. Thus, to leave a child outside to die from exposure was not viewed as murder, but rather a refusal to let them into society.

Abortion was often attempted, but it was very risky and often killed both the mother and the baby. Thus, in ancient Rome unwanted pregnancies were often delivered and the child was left to die on the local trash heap. Sometimes slave traders would come and get the children (usually the boys) for future slave trade. Others would take the girls (and boys) and raise them in a life of prostitution.

The early Christian community followed the Jewish custom of forbidding abortion and infanticide. God was the giver of life, and life was to be guarded and valued as a gift from above, not something to be traded or bartered with.

Therefore, the Christians of the first and second century had a golden opportunity to act on their beliefs. The good always wins over the bad, just as water always wins over fire. The world around them threw their unwanted babies on the trash heap and nobody thought it was strange. What did the Christians do?

The babies on the trash heaps were called riff-raff. Nobody cared about them. Except the Christians. The Christians decided to adopt these "unwanted" children into their own homes and raise them as they would their own. This practice became such a well-known phenomena that many Romans derided the Christians for their silly practices. The Romans denounced this practice as well as the entire Christian faith.

Justin Martyr, a Christian apologist, argued that "unwanted" persons were exactly the kind of people that Christians wanted to be involved with, just as Christ had been.

Some things never change. The world is currently home to 39 million unwanted children, and many of these precious miracles will never experience the love of Christ through adoption. If you know Christ you have been adopted into God's family. You know how precious it is.

The early Christians had considerably less means to provide for the riff-raff children than we do today. Adoption is not easy; it never was. Riff-raff children can be smelly, dirty, sickly, or callous. But they are more beautiful and valuable than all the heavens and earths. They are, through love, created as eternal souls. Why don't you adopt?

Faith is Believing
Suzan Hudspeth

My dad recently had a heart attack. He was in the critical care unit for eight days and then in the hospital for another three weeks.

Having diabetes made his prognosis poor because his heart and kidneys were not functioning properly to begin with. It seemed each small improvement was met with a larger set-back. When he finally came home, the doctors told us that he was very weak and would probably not get better. They didn't know how long he would live, but he would never fully recover.

My nine-year-old daughter knew I was upset. I tried to prepare her for what we believed was the inevitable, by telling her that we should check on Papaw often and show him we loved him because he might not be around a for a long time.

She took this very seriously. She requested prayer at church for her Papaw and we prayed for him every night. Once she even went down to the front of the church to be anointed for him.Shortly after that, we were at dad's house one afternoon, and he seemed really sick. Immediately, my daughter went to get the pastor, who lived next door, to come and pray for him.

After my father endured another bout in the hospital with congestive heart failure, I again tried to explain that Papaw was very ill and that Jesus might take him to heaven soon. She quickly said, "But Mom, God's gonna heal him 'cause we've been praying for him."

Looking back, I am ashamed by my lack of faith.

22

Today, my father has made a remarkable recovery. The doctors are amazed when he walks in, unassisted, to his appointments and sits and visits with them. He has exceeded any goals they ever set for him. The Bible tells us there are times when we must become as little children. I look at my daughter and thank God every day for her faith and dedication to Christ.

Although there were a lot of people praying for my dad, I am convinced that she truly touched heaven with her prayers and with a faith that her prayers would be answered. In life, I will teach her many things, but none so important as the lesson she taught me. She taught me that faith is believing!

His Timing Still Amazes
Roland and Sue Stirnemann

Our story is a story of hope, for those who have been married many years and have given up on becoming parents.

It actually begins over 20 years ago. After being married in 1981, we decided to spend the first five years or so just getting to know each other.

It was when we decided to start having children that our infertility problems surfaced. Because the problems were untreatable at the time, we focused on the ministry we were involved in, instead of what we could do nothing about.

It was another 10 years before we again pursued parenthood, only to discover natural childbearing would never happen for us.

We researched adoption from every angle (domestic, international, special needs) and came to the depressing conclusion that the two of us would just grow old together – without children.

We committed ourselves to spoiling our nieces and nephews as if they were our own children. It's not that adoption wasn't possible for us, but the emotional rollercoaster of ups and downs during the pursuit and waiting period seemed too heavy to bear.

It was when we had totally given up the idea of ever being parents that God stepped up to the plate. His timing still amazes me!

24

If we couldn't be parents we decided we would plunge ourselves even more into the work of the Lord. We put our house up for sale at top dollar as a type of fleece (similar to what Gideon did). If the house sold at that high price, we would trust that it was the Lord's leading for us to move to Florida to help out in a small home-mission church. The house sold in just a few weeks!

We were ecstatic about moving although we knew it was a huge step of faith. After all, God had sent a buyer so His hand had to be in it.

Two days after signing the seller's purchase agreement, the phone rang – changing our lives forever. His timing still amazes me!

How our old file surfaced – I'll never understand. . . We had not attempted to contact New Beginnings in over two years!

During that life-changing phone call we were told that a child was to be born in about five months and that our profile was a perfect match. They then asked if we were still interested in adopting?

God changed our Florida plans.

Everything became clear. We scrambled to prepare for the new arrival; finding another house, getting our home study and picking out names. His timing still amazes me!

A few months later we received the call that our little bundle of joy had finally arrived. We named our little boy Jeremy, which means, "God will arise."

When it seemed like our future was destined to be an empty nest, God "arose" to the occasion and filled our home with the laughter (and crying!) of a tiny new life.

Every now and then I look at all the toys strewn across the floor and just smile (well…sometimes cry). The home that was once kept spotless was invaded by a lively mess-making little person and we wouldn't trade it for anything. His timing still amazes me!

A few days after bringing Jeremy home, I was feeding him in a rocker, tears running down my cheeks, when inspiration began bubbling up inside me. I quickly grabbed a pen and paper and in the next few minutes the following poured forth from my heart and soul.

Just when we thought the door to parenthood had slammed firmly shut in our faces, your tiny hand reached out through our emptiness clutching the key to our hearts.

Every time I look into your bouncing eyes I'm amazed how God entrusted us with you.

Remembering the unanswered questions and hurts of the past gets harder with each passing moment that I spend holding you in my arms, watching you peacefully sleep.

Even when you cry, when you're hungry or need a diaper change, I can't stop myself from smiling at the thought of how great a blessing God bestowed upon us by placing you in our care.

Many changes have already taken place in our home and lives, and many more will surely occur, but we are ready, and

in some cases even anxious, for the changes you will force upon our lifestyle.

You will probably never be able to fully comprehend what your introduction into our lives at this point in time means to us, but know this, Jeremy Roland, to your Mom and Dad, you are the physical evidence that our God is able to do anything.

Thank you New Beginnings. His timing still amazes me!

A Story from Germany
Christina Brantner

Adoption of African American boys by an older, single foreigner?

"Oh, no!" You might say worriedly.

"Aber ja!" The two boys would chuckle in German, "Oh yes!"

After a wonderful career in academics and a workaholic, fun and industrious life for my university and no mate to be found, I consider myself very lucky indeed to be able to enjoy this great family life of ours.

And academia is giving me something back after all these working years, the flexibility to raise kids as an unhurried single parent.

We live in a big old, clunky house with lots of children's books, three cats, a big sandbox in a very English garden and toys scattered over three floors.

Our "house language" is German – after all, why teach my boys English with an accent if they can learn a foreign language accent-free?

And the "father" question so far has been a mute one, especially since we have very involved and young godfathers who tumble and bike with the boys or attend "father's night" at pre-school.

Four and a half years ago when, I first held my oldest son in my arms on a sunny January day in Tupelo, I fell in love as only a mother can.

Benjamin is a tall, bubbly preschooler now who in many ways is like me: interested in language games, loves to bake and loves to laugh – but is also very much not like me: not just his darker skin, but his very analytical, logical mind, his ease with people and his eternally good mood. Besides giving my life an anchor and a purpose, he gives me a new appreciation for learning with an unprejudiced fresh and inquisitive mind! What a gift he is giving me day after day! And then people say how lucky he is to be sharing my lifestyle – well I always say that I am equally lucky!

And then in January of 2002, little Nikolas joined us, because I felt I was focusing so very much on Benjamin that it became unhealthy for him AND me.

Also, as an older and white adoptive parent, and after having read an awful lot about race issues in this country and this world, I decided it would be better for my first child to have another child to go through life with him when maybe I won't quite "get" a slight or when I won't be there to wipe away a tear, then at least brother would be there!

They are still very much at the beginning of their relationship and love for one another, but it is a strong very strong one from day one.

I had told my two and a half-year-old that a baby was growing in a birthmother's tummy and one day we'd get the phone call, get on a plane and pick up our much-awaited baby.

29

It happened just like that, and when six-day-old Nikolas was brought into the agency room where Benjamin and I were waiting, Benjamin screamed these heart-felt words "our baby, our baby!"

He has been a very protective and loving big brother ever since – even through the months of disability of Nikolas when Benjamin had to play second fiddle most times.

Yes, talk about the worst nightmare, when you believe that your child will be perfectly healthy and then, at 10 months of age, a tracheotomy is performed that leaves a breathing tube in your child. The situation required 24/7 professional care that insurance did not cover. But with the help of many friends and prayers we got through those eight months and a major operation to reconstruct Niki's airway – and he is now a happy, healthy, talking and laughing boy of 19 months.

Adoption has changed our lives forever. My parents, who live in Germany, finally have grandchildren to dote on. I'm in a win-win situation and the boys will have two cultures to shape their minds and enrich their lives.

Every three years we live in Berlin for a semester, as I take my students on a semester abroad and, of course, my boys go to a German preschool and later on – school.

Adoption in Germany is much more difficult to do; a single person who's slightly over 40 would not be eligible. Thus, my boys and I will be eternally grateful to America because she enabled us to come together and share our bountiful love for one another.

Into My Heart
Anonymous

One crisp fall day, our adopted daughter was riding in the car with my mother. With a grownup tone to her three-year-old voice she asked, "Nana, does Jesus live in your heart?"

My mother, suddenly very proud of my spiritual parenting said, "Yes! Yes, He does!"

Very interested in any topic of conversation that didn't include Blue's Clues, my mother adjusted the mirror so that she could see the sweet face of her granddaughter riding in her car seat in the back.

"He lives in my heart too," my little girl said with great pride.

Not wanting to giggle, but yet so touched, my mother met the gaze of her granddaughter through the rear-view mirror and said, "I am so glad to hear that."

"Yea, but I didn't swallow Him. Did you?"

It's a God-Thing
Anonymous

As I was writing a check at Wal-Mart, the clerk was observing my children. She said, "What a pretty little girl. What a handsome young man."

I smiled and looked at my children. They are so very different.

My daughter has blond curly hair, deep brown eyes and round cherub-like cheeks. My son has rich brownish red hair and chiseled European features.

As I looked at him, his light green eyes latched onto mine. He rolled his eyes as if to say, "Can you believe she thinks I am handsome?"

I smiled from ear to ear! I had to agree with her. But instead of pointing out how right she was I simply said, "Thank you."

Now looking directly at me she was suddenly confused. She looked at my daughter, then my son. Then she returned her gaze to me. She said, "How is it none of you look alike?"

My heart skipped a beat. I suddenly felt defensive as if my motherhood were being questioned. I looked at her and stammering said, "My children are adopted."

"Oh, that's so wonderful!" She said as she took my check and handed me a receipt.

As we walked to the car, I asked my eleven-year-old son if he'd prefer that I not tell strangers that he and his sister were adopted when they notice our physical differences.

In his laid-back manner he shrugged and was very quiet until we reached the car.

Then as he handed me the grocery sacks he said, "You know Mom, when people ask why we look different, we could just tell them, 'It's a God-thing!'"

Just Another Special Family
Kelly & Trish Kermoade

We had been married for several years and were unable to have children.

After a long search, we decided to apply through New Beginnings in order to adopt an infant. Because of unique circumstances, before we got through the whole application process, a child was born and might be available to us. While we were hastily working to get everything done, the birthmother decided to parent her baby.

In January 1999, Debbie Velie called to say she had a little boy who had been born a few days earlier. She wanted to know if we were interested. He was five weeks early, and we were very interested!

We arrived in Tupelo at 7:00 pm a few days later and Debbie and Tom Velie came to our motel, bringing with them our precious little boy. He was so tiny. It was awesome to hold that little baby. We just sat around looking at him that evening. The first night I could hardly sleep as I kept waking up to make sure that he was still breathing!

It was wonderful to have our little boy, but the legal and interstate procedure didn't go very quickly - we're told this is common.

Thankfully, we found minister friends, the Andersons, living about 15 miles from Tupelo and were able to pass some of the time with them. They were excited for us and even joined us in court. After about a three week delay, we were able to leave Mississippi with him! But it was worth it!

Our little boy is now four-and-a-half-years-old and very busy. He loves to play ball and ride his bike. He likes to play the drums and is very good. He always asks, "Mommy, do you like my new beat?"

At about age two, his daddy broke his leg at work. Our son had to prop his leg up just like Daddy and even had to use a cane when Daddy did.

When he was three, we were outside playing baseball. I was pitching to him and he finally said, "Mommy, I better pitch, you're not doing very good!"

Having a son has certainly broadened my horizons when it comes to sports.

At age four, as he was throwing a paper towel in the trash, he told me he was going to make a "dam slunk!"

He thinks when a person says they are dizzy that they are saying "busy." So several times he has told me, "Mommy, I'm busy (meaning dizzy)."

Lots of times when telling Daddy goodnight, he'll say, "I love you, Daddy. Have a good night. Be careful driving to work. Don't hit any deer. Have a good day at work."

When our son was two-and-a-half, we went through the adoption application process again and six months later a little girl was born who would join our family through adoption. This adoption wasn't nearly as complicated as our first one. We were able to go to court and finalize the adoption after only two days.

She is now 18-months-old, beautiful and even busier than her brother. It is so sweet to see her go up to her brother and give him a hug and kiss.

There are times though when she pulls his hair and his ear too!

Our daughter always liked her pacifier. We always called it "pacifier" instead of "binky." She began calling it "fier" which sounds like "fire." One day after we were trying to break her from the "fier" she saw another baby with one and said, "I want fier."

There is a song that I often sing to the kids. It is so cute to hear my daughter singing along with me. You can't understand most words, but you know she is singing the song. Many times she just starts singing that little song.

Both of our children like music and love for us to read to them. They like to play outside and to take walks. They're just "normal" kids.

One of the best things we've experienced is when the children begin to put their arms around your neck and hug you! It is wonderful to be called Daddy and Mommy when you thought it might never happen.

Many people think they look alike and they act like brother and sister too. Sometimes people folks will ask if they are brother and sister. I always say, "Not until we got them."

Little Lightning
Michael and Jennifer Johnson

We knew, even before we were married, that conceiving a child might be difficult for us. Adoption was always in our thoughts and we talked about it almost from the beginning. I think we both knew in our heart of hearts that God's plan all along was for us to adopt a child.

We tried for several years to conceive, but all attempts failed. Some people talk about what a difficult decision adoption is. For us it was like coming home. We knew this was God's will and we embraced it.

In January of 2001, we sent a letter to our entire family letting them know about our plans to adopt and asking for their prayers and support for our child, the child's birthmother and for ourselves.

Not long after that we started all of the paperwork with New Beginnings.

In 2001, we received our acceptance letter telling us that we had been approved by New Beginnings and had been placed on the waiting list! We settled back and resigned ourselves to a long wait.

Our wait was not nearly as long as we had anticipated and in early 2002, we received a call from Debbie Velie.

A baby boy had been born three days earlier and she was offering him to us! We worked frantically to complete the final home study visit so we could pick up our baby.

Our world turned upside down and inside out overnight!

We flew into action. I remember absolutely shaking with anticipation and energy. We had a son! My heart soared! Our prayers had been answered and our wait was almost over. Just a few more days.

After we finally stopped crying, laughing and screaming in joy we started calling everyone. Our families were stunned and thrilled and amazed all at the same time.

Questions about our little boy flew across the phone lines. What? When? Where? How? We answered those questions over and over again. I feel as though I should have gotten a "Thank You for Driving our Stock Price Up" note from the phone company for that month: we certainly sent them enough business.

Our family and friends rejoiced with us. I will never forget calling my mother and telling her that she was a grandmother. She was shocked!

Then I called my best friend, Kimberly, and told her that I was a mom. She didn't believe me at first. I don't believe we have ever been so excited in our lives.

My friend Kimberly went with me on a shopping expedition that evening. We bought a car seat, a pack and play, baby clothes, diapers, formula, bath items, toys, and the list goes on. We raced through Toys-R-Us and Wal-mart. We were on a mission. We shopped until we dropped. And the whole time, I don't think my feet ever touched the ground.

But, we also had to complete the "dreaded" home study visit. Not really knowing what to expect, I stayed up all night cleaning. I dusted in places surely no one would ever think to look. I wanted to make sure everything was perfect. We moved furniture and vacuumed and cleaned out cabinets to make sure everything was baby-proofed---even though it would be months before our child was old enough to get into anything. He was only three days old, after all. But I had to make sure!

Debbie Velie arrived the next day for our home visit. It was not at all what I expected. She kept it personal and friendly—we weren't going to end up in prison. She didn't even check under my sofa to make sure it had been vacuumed – after all that hard work!

Debbie was a great joy to work with, but I must admit that I let out a huge sigh of relief once she left after telling us our home had passed with flying colors! The real test was still yet to come---meeting our son.

We arrived at the New Beginning's offices the next day just before noon. We were so nervous! Not long after we arrived our son's foster mom brought him in.

There are no words to describe that moment when Samuel was placed in my arms for the very first time. I was in awe of him. He was so tiny. He was so perfect in every way. And, as I am sure every new mother does, I counted ten tiny fingers and ten tiny toes. I gently stroked his beautiful little head of reddish blonde hair.

And when he looked at me for the first time with those pure blue eyes, I knew I would never let go of him! I knew right then that I was holding a miracle. God's miracle. God's presence was very palpable at that moment.

Becoming a new mom and dad so suddenly doesn't allow time to properly prepare you for those first few moments of parenting - nothing does.

After rocking Sam for a little while and then feeding him a bottle for the first time, I felt it would be a good idea to change his diaper and then he would be all nice and cozy to take a nap on the drive to my mom's house.

I got all the necessary items ready—changing pad, diaper, wipes, powder, etc. I had them all neatly arranged. After fumbling with snaps and Velcro I finally had the old diaper off and was getting the new diaper unfolded and ready to put on my young son.

No one warned me that you must change boys with lightening speed. Before I could properly secure the new diaper my little miracle decided this would be a good time to poop!

I was shocked and appalled that my little boy would initiate me in such a way. Poop went everywhere! What a mess! And, I had an audience to boot. Changing a diaper for the first time should not be a public event! Everyone was laughing at my antics of trying to clean up the mess and get things covered before anything else decided to escape! Even worse, it was caught on camera! I will never live that down.

I am proud to say, though, that I have gotten much better at diaper changes. I can do them at the speed-of-light now!

Those first few days with Sam are etched forever in my heart and mind. There is nothing in the world like becoming a mom and a dad. The bond between a mother and her child is undeniable.

And, I am happy to say that the bond just gets stronger with each day and parenting Sam gets more enjoyable each day. He is almost two now and is the light of our lives. I can't believe sometimes how much he has grown. Our family is so blessed by Sam. He has brought untold joy to us time after time after time.

Born in My Heart
Chelsea's Mom & Dad (Linda and Darry)

We can remember the day we were introduced to our daughter, Chelsea, as vividly as if it were yesterday. That was one of the most wonderful days of our lives! We can't begin to explain all the emotions we felt that day. We thought Chelsea was the most beautiful baby we had ever seen and we loved her very much even before we saw her.

The whole day, which included the court meeting and our eleven-hour trip back home, was filled with joy and excitement.

It has been nearly nine years since we brought Chelsea home and she continues to add so much joy and meaning to our lives.

Looking back, one of our first concerns was whether or not she would love and bond with us. In support groups we heard stories of how either the adoptive parents or the child had problems bonding.

We had non-stop visitors during the first three days that she was home. In the midst of all the excitement, we noticed that when someone was holding her and either my husband or I would talk, she would turn her head toward us. At first we thought it was our imagination, but other people noticed it as well.

By the end of the second day, she would cry when she wanted one of us to hold her. She already knew who we were and had bonded with us! We felt this was a miracle and a confirmation that God had made this wonderful baby just for us!

We had discussed how and when we thought would be the best time to tell Chelsea that she was adopted.

Well, things don't always work out as planned. Chelsea bombarded us with questions long before we were ready for them.

It began when a mother of one of the children in my home daycare became pregnant. Chelsea, who was three years old at the time, asked why her tummy was getting bigger. I explained that there was a baby growing in there. Chelsea thought that was so exciting and wanted to know how it felt when she was in MY tummy! At first, I ignored her, but she kept asking me day after day.

We finally decided we had to tell her the truth and to "normalize" adoption. The next time she asked, I told her that something was wrong and my tummy couldn't have babies in it. I explained to her that she actually grew in someone else's tummy.

She thought this over for a moment, and then blurted, "Mommy, that means that she gave me away! How could anyone give their baby away! Didn't that girl love me?"

I could not believe these questions were coming from a three-year old child! I explained to her that her birth-mom loved her very much. In fact, it was her great love for Chelsea that influenced her to proceed with the adoption.

I told her that there are times when some girls are not ready or able to take the responsibility of being a mommy. I explained that her birth-mom was very special to us. I tried to help her understand that God never makes mistakes. When He made Chelsea, He had a perfect plan already in place.

Chelsea has had more questions since that day, and we know she will have other issues later (just like every child does), but we always have been and will continue to be honest with her. She is now proud of this fact and will occasionally tell people that she is adopted.

When God answers a prayer, He always knows just how to fit everything together so beautifully. She is so much more than what we prayed for.

One of the added blessings is how much she looks like me and even has the same interests and personality traits. People, often strangers, have approached me just to say how much we look alike. I have gone to school functions where parents, students and teachers have introduced themselves to me and then say, "You must be Chelsea's mom."

Our adoption was a positive experience, but it did not come easily. We had to go through so many losses.

First of all, after trying all the medical procedures (which were unsuccessful), we had to accept the fact that we would not have our own biological children. Speaking from a woman's standpoint, it was extremely difficult for me to accept that.

Then, the adoption process is not always an easy road to take. We researched our options and found more closed doors than open ones. But now, looking back, we can actually thank God for all the losses and heartaches because if we had physically had a child, we would not have adopted Chelsea. We simply cannot imagine our lives without her.

We have always told her that she is our "Gift from Heaven." Our lives have been and continue to be blessed and enriched because of her. We thank God every day for New Beginnings, her birth-mom, and, of course, our precious daughter.

Forever Families and Our Forever Father: A Few Short Stories
From a Mother of the Heart

- I -

The other day, I was eating lunch at K-Mart. Iit is amazing where we will eat for love - with my daughter who is three-and-a-half years old.

We saw a friend of ours whose son, Graham, who had suffered from leukemia.

My daughter asked who the lady was and when I told her that it was Graham's mother.

She said, "Mother we prayed for Graham and God healed him."

I told her that she was right and said, Isn't God Awesome?"

She smiled and said, "He is Awesome and he has Powers, Good, Powers!"

I was amazed at the faith and deep understanding of a child. Not a day goes by that our girls (yes, we have adopted two beautiful daughters) cease to amaze me.

They bring such joy to our lives and they teach me so much about loving life. God is so good! All we have to do is to look and listen to the faith of a child to understand the love, grace, and power of our Almighty Father.

46

- II -

We want our children to feel proud of who they are and understand adoption as a natural way of becoming a family.

Our church has been blessed with expectant mothers and recently our oldest daughter, Hannah, asked if she came from Mommy's belly.

We explained to her that Mommy was not able to carry a baby in her belly and that God had sent her special to our family. We told Hannah, that we had prayed that God would send us children and that Miss Debbie Velie had helped us pray that God would send us the right angels for our family.

She smiled and said that when she grew up that she didn't want to have a baby the way Mrs. Merritt (our friend from church) had a baby, but that she wanted God to send her baby special like she was scnt.

We tell her that we are her "Forever Family" and that God makes people families in many different ways. She seems to be satisfied with this explanation.

- III -

I spent the longest time last night watching my two daughters sleep. During this time, my heart became full of love and awe at the gift that God had given. My husband and I silently thanked God for our girls.

My thoughts began to turn to their birthmothers and I prayed that God would allow them to know how loved that their girls were.

It is amazing how joined we are to them by God's grace. We have both been so blessed that God has given us this beautiful child.

It is only through his grace that a birthmother can so selflessly give their child life and then love them enough to share them with parents to raise.

It is also only through God's grace that the adoptive family can receive such a glorious gift and know that they will be able to love and shepherd their child to be the adult that God would have them be. God's power is so evident when I look at our girls.

That God could have known before our girls were ever born that we would be the perfect people to raise them amazes me.

People have asked me, if I am sad that I was unable to give birth to children and, honestly, before receiving our girls my answer would have been yes. However, today, I would not trade having my girls for being able to give birth. Our children were perfectly made by God for us and were just brought to us through unconventional means.

I hope that anyone that is considering adoption realizes that these children are theirs because they are a gift from God. All children, whether ours by birth or through adoption, are God's children given to their parents as a gift.

Sometimes God gives you the miracle you ask for, but he gives it to you how He knows will be best.

I can only say, "Thank you God for unanswered prayers and for the joy we now know might have been missed if you had not guided us to your will and wonderful way!"

- IV -

One of the most embarrassing moments that we have had with our 3-year-old daughter happened when we had taken her with us to the beauty shop.

A woman with thinning hair was having her hair styled. The stylist was working a hairpiece into the women's hair to make it appear thicker. About that time, our Hannah said in a very loud voice, "I have a hat, but I left it at home."

I was so embarrassed, but the women laughed and said, "Well, I guess it does look like a hat." You never know what children in all of their unbridled honesty will say.

- V -

Our oldest daughter, Hannah, was recently visiting her grandparents. When she visits, Hannah loves to go out to their farm and see the goats and horse. On one of those day trips, she and her Grandfather found one of the goats dead. This upset Hannah and she cried. They buried the goat and said a prayer.

When Hannah got home she began to ask many questions about death. I told her that if we ask God into our heart, and believed in him, that when we die God gives us heavenly bodies and that these bodies do not feel any pain or worry.

One night while I was reading her bedtime story, she looked at me and said, "Mom, when we die and get our heavenly bodies, mine is going to sparkle."

I could not help but be tickled at the wondrous mind of a child. What a joy our girls have brought to our lives.

Life Processing with Lily
Jack & Lori Yonts

The Mushroom Story

Children, whether or not they join a family through the process of adoption, enjoy defining their history…their "story." Lily is no different and she *does* have an explanation for everything.

Wild mushrooms grow rapidly in a slightly boggy spot on the north side of our home. Our oldest daughter, Lily, could conquer the world, while her Uncle Danny - unfortunately for him - is paranoid about everything. This includes mushrooms!

On one particularly 'mushroom-favorable day,' Lily and Gabriella escorted their uncle to the Valley of the Mushrooms. Danny immediately began instructing the girls, "Don't you dare eat these mushrooms. They're poisonous! Don't get anywhere near them!"

Little Lily (who was adopted at birth and has no recollection or knowledge of her history), straight-faced and with her best *"I know the answers to everything in life"* voice decided that it was time to share a portion of her infinite knowledge. "Did you know that my birthfather ate poisonous mushrooms and died? That is why I was adopted by Mom and Dad."

From "Debbie's Belly"

Several months after expounding on the "demise" of her birthfather after he, reportedly, ate poisonous mushrooms, Lily added to her voluminous 'Lily's Encyclopedia of Modern Civilization' by sharing her birthmother's history.

50

Lily was overheard explaining to her little sister Gabriella, why they weren't "nursed by Mom like their cousins." In a hushed and serious tone, she told Gabriella that they were actually born to Miss Debbie (Director of Client Services at New Beginnings).

"Yes," she said, "Miss Debbie is the mother of hundreds of babies like us and she finds other wonderful people, like Mom and Dad, to help her take care of them."

Lily loves Miss Debbie and what better explanation than to "become Debbie's daughter by birth." Congratulations on those "hundreds of babies," Miss Debbie!

My Dad's Deer Hunting

Jack loves to hunt—in his spare time. So, whenever he would be away from his church on a business trip and saints would ask where he was, Lily was quick to answer, "He's deer hunting!"

Playing in the Basement

Lily has a playroom in the basement and loves to spend time there playing with her toys, dolls and her play kitchen.

One Friday while her parents were getting ready to leave for a weekend trip, Lily was happily playing in the basement. When the family was ready to leave, they called for Lily and she ran upstairs and off they went.

When the family returned home the next week and walked in the house, a terrible odor assaulted them. They quickly searched the house for the cause of the smell. Not finding anything on the main floor, they made their way to the basement.

To their dismay, they discovered that Lily had taken all the meat from the freezer when she was playing with her mini kitchen. Thawed meat and a very smelly mess was everywhere, necessitating removing carpet, throwing out toys, etc.

Lily learned that the meat in the freezer should stay in the freezer!

Our Adoption Story
Jason, Davinna and MacKenzie Grace Reeves

The story of Kenzie's Adoption begins long before she came to be a part of our family and even before she was ever conceived.

Jeremiah 1:5 says, *Before I formed thee in the belly I knew thee; and before thou camest forth out of the womb I sanctified thee?*

We have always known that God had a divine plan for our lives, for our marriage, and for our family. What we did not always know was what that plan was.

Jason and I met in 1995. We developed a close friendship over the next year and began dating in 1996. Jason and I poured our hearts out to each other and often discussed plans for our future. These discussions always seemed to lead back to our love of family. Jason and I both came from very loving and close-knit, Christian families so it was only natural that we would someday want a family of our own.

Our wedding in October 1996 seemed like the perfect fairy tale. Marrying Jason was a dream come true. I could not have imagined that we would not be conceiving a child of our own quite soon.

After being married for several months, we decided to start our family. After trying for over a year to conceive, I went to our physician, Dr. Janice H. with my concerns.

Dr. H. felt that it was time to start testing to see if there were any health issues for Jason or myself that would prevent conception.

It did not take long to discover that there were reproductive problems.

We had been praying for God's will in all of these tests. I remember the devastation that I felt when we started getting those test results. However, we were blessed to have such a wonderful friend in Dr. H. She told me that all was not lost. She said, "Davinna, you can always adopt."

I left her office that day and cried and prayed all the way home. I remember sharing the results with Jason that night and he confirmed the words that Dr. H. had said to me.

Jason held me and told me, "Maybe there is a reason that we cannot have children. Maybe there is a child out there who needs us."

I wish that I could tell you that I was ready to accept this plan right then and there but, I cannot. At my insistence, we continued to seek medical treatment for our infertility. We saw fertility specialists around the state hoping for different results, but the results never changed.

We continued to pray and seek guidance from the Lord, and from the pastor and pastor's wife. We also decided to use this time to further our careers. I returned to college and completed the requirements for certification and licensure as a respiratory therapist. Jason decided to fulfill his dream of becoming a police officer and went to work in the local sheriff's office, while awaiting the opportunity to go to the police academy.

We had come to somewhat of a standstill in what my father-in-law would come to call "The Great Baby Acquisition."

One weekend, we went to church to find that we had some very special guests visiting from Wisconsin. We met Lily and Gabriella. I immediately fell in love with these girls and their stories touched my heart in a way that it had never been touched before.

Although I had grown up knowing their mom, Lori, we had lost contact over the years. After the service, I approached Lori and asked her how she and Jack had come to adopt Lily and Gabriella.

Lori then told me about New Beginnings. She told me that Debbie Velie could prove to be one of my most valued friends. Lori told me that they had worked with another agency, but that New Beginnings would be the one to use above any other agency out there.

She told me, "If Debbie tells you that something is going to be a certain way - that is exactly how it will be. Debbie will be up-front with you."

Jason and I talked about it again and contacted New Beginnings for information. Within a couple of days, the packet of information was in our mailbox.

We told our families that we were going to try to adopt and they were very supportive. I remember calling Jason's dad, Jim, and asking him if he was ready to be a grandfather.

He got so excited and asked, "When?"

I answered, "About two to four years."

He said, "What are you? A pachyderm?"

55

I laughed and told him that we were going to adopt.

During the time that we were working on getting all of our paperwork completed and getting approved, Jim became ill.

We had several conversations with him regarding the adoption process. It was during one of these conversations that he helped us choose the name for our precious daughter.

By May 2002, we knew that our daughter would be, MacKenzie Grace.

When we started the adoption process, we wondered how we would ever be able to afford the adoption fee. Once again, we were knocking on the doors of heaven and asking for help. We found that when you serve such a mighty God, He is always there to meet your needs.

Someone gave us the name of a lady who makes candles in the basement of her home. We got candles from her and sold them. We probably sold enough candles to light the entire southeastern United States of America. One lady who purchased a candle from us paid $100 for that one candle.

We took orders for cakes and my mother baked them and we sold them. I delivered one cake to a nurse who gave me a check for $100 for it.

My parents needed some repairs on their van. When they went to pick the van up, the repair bill was $500, the mechanic told them to take that $500 and put it in our adoption fund. We had many family members and friends who gave what they could afford to us to put towards Kenzie's adoption fees.

During this time, we lost Jim. Jason was the sole heir to Jim's estate and we put a large portion of his inheritance in the adoption account as well.

Just when we thought we could not wait any longer, we got the call that we had been waiting for.

In October 2003, Tom Velie called from New Beginnings and asked permission to share our profile with a New Beginning's birthmother.

Over the period of a couple of weeks, Mackenzie's birthmother reviewed our profile and eventually chose us.

Debbie Velie helped set up a phone call between Mackenzie's birthmom and me. I was so nervous when I first spoke to *Karen on the phone.

One of the first questions that she asked was, "What does being a mother mean to you?"

I told her, "Right now, my entire world hinges on your decision. Being a mother means everything to me."

Karen and I talked for several hours before she explained her question to me. She told me, "This baby does not need two moms; she needs one set of parents. You and Jason will be her parents."

I asked her what she was in this relationship then and she told me, "I am simply the vessel that God has chosen to deliver your child to you in. I believe that my role is to be her sister in Christ."

57

Debbie told me later that Karen requested that I get to be in the delivery room with her. She said that Karen wanted Kenzie to be held by her mom first. I was so happy that Karen could call me Kenzie's mom!

In November 2003, Nana, Granddaddy, and I headed to Tupelo to await the arrival of our precious baby girl. Jason was not able to take very much time off work so we decided that he would join us when we knew that MacKenzie was on her way.

We waited in Tupelo for a week before MacKenzie was born.

Karen's labor was induced. I don't think that those nurses had ever heard as much praying as we did in the delivery room that day.

Once again, God answered prayer and Karen's labor went smoothly and MacKenzie Grace was born quickly and with ease.

MacKenzie came into the world waving her left arm as if to say, "Hey everybody, I am here!"

As soon as she was born, I began crying. I thought the tears would never end. All I could think was, "You gorgeous baby. You are my child." There was more love in my heart than I ever imagined I could feel. Any doubts that I had about adoption vanished immediately. I knew, without a doubt, that this was my daughter, my precious baby girl.

By the grace of God, I was able to hand her back to Karen and know that she would love her enough to share her with us and to allow Jason and I to provide a life for MacKenzie that she could not give.

When they took Kenzie to the nursery, I discovered that Jason had arrived while his daughter was being born. I had always known that Jason would be a wonderful and loving father to our daughter, but I could never imagine the love that was on his face the first time that he saw her and held her. It was such a tender and sweet expression.

MacKenzie just reached up and grabbed his thumb and held it so tight. While she was holding his thumb, she was wrapping herself right around his heart. Jason began calling her, "Daddy's Little Princess" the day that she was born and she continues to be his little princess.

The hospital policy was such that we could only see MacKenzie in Karen's hospital room. During one of our visits with Karen, she told me that she needed to share something with me.

She said, "Don't ever let anyone tell you that you did not go through labor for this baby. All of those prayers that you prayed for her and all of those tears that you cried because you could not have a child, those were labor pains. All of the times that you thought your heart would break because you could not bear to see that mother pushing her child through the mall in the stroller and all of those times when friends told you that they were pregnant and you wanted so desperately to be happy for them but could not, those were labor pains. You experienced spiritual labor for her. You're every bit as much of a mother to her as anyone else is to their child."

Mississippi law requires a 72-hour waiting period before a birthparent is allowed to sign parental release forms. MacKenzie was released from the hospital two days after she was born and, because both Karen and the birthfather signed parental release forms, we were able to secure a fully completed adoption decree before leaving for home.

Once again, I showered MacKenzie's face with tears. We knew without a doubt that she was finally legally our daughter.

Today, it is hard to imagine our lives without MacKenzie Grace. She is truly an answer to prayer.

My mother-in-law, Kenzie's Mimi, likes to say that if we lined up all the little baby girls in the world, we could not have chosen a more perfect angel to complete our family. It goes without saying that MacKenzie is loved by her Nana and Granddaddy, as well as her Mimi and Granddaddy and her aunts, uncles, cousins, and great grandparents.

People often ask us if we will tell MacKenzie that she is adopted and we tell them that she will grow up with that knowledge daily.

She is often told Kenzie's story as a bedtime story and we pray daily for sweet and precious Karen.

Children have different ways that they come to be a part of a family, some by birth, some by fostering, and some by adoption. Adoption just happens to be the vehicle that God chose to place Kenzie Grace in our family.

*Karen – not her real name. Karen, Jason and Davinna chose to work together for an open adoption. We have not found these to be the norm, but they do work if the parties are fully informed and in complete agreement as to the boundaries and expectations.

Had I Been Rosemary
Kimberlee Medicine Horn Jackson

I sit across from my Dad at his favorite table in Arby's restaurant.

Eighty–two years has stooped him over to a right angle. It is hard for me to see these physical changes in him. Now he walks with a cane - accepting the need for it.

His eyes are like the sky reflecting off fresh winter snow. They are beautiful eyes that show the unmistakable, unique glow of faith, impossible to hide.

We talk over coffee left too long on the warming plate and apple turnovers drizzled with icing. We are the first and only customers here.

I listen patiently as he remembers other conversations with fondness, spoken with friends who no longer walk this earth. He boldly states he wants to live to be 100. As long as God wakes him each morning there is work to be done.

We talk about my brothers and sister who are all adopted and pray for those needing salvation and for others just beginning to grow wings of faith.

He leans closer to me and says out of all his kids I am the one he can talk to about these things.

I share with dad the search for my birthmother and my questions as to why it all happened.

Pieces of the puzzle seem to fit together at the oddest moments. Just recently mom told me the first Indian child they tried to adopt didn't work out because the mother changed her mind at the last minute. The child's name was Rosemary.

I wonder how her life turned out. As an adopted child, I have always wondered how life would have been on the reservation. I am startled to know I almost never made it here.

Dad listens with the patience and love of a father having seen his daughter grow from a toddler to a mother.

A fleeting image fills my mind: how he caught me on a speeding bike when I forgot how to work the breaks. He saved me from crashing into the back wall of the garage. I still see the look on his face as he braces himself for the impact.

"You are here Kim because this is where God wants you to be." He sums up the unanswered questions. I've read that in the Bible.

I feel joy in the simplicity of his feelings from the heart. I have taken another step in accepting God's plan for me.

I realize with new clarity how much I'd have missed had I been Rosemary.

Our Story with New Beginnings
David and Vicki Jensen

Many years ago we both knew we wanted a baby in our lives. Unfortunately it was not God's plan for us to give birth to that baby. We tried unsuccessfully for several years to get pregnant. We finally decided God was telling us that our family was meant to be grown through adoption and not through birth.

During this same time, my wife's sister and her husband were also deciding that adoption was the way to build their family. They applied to New Beginnings and six months later had a beautiful baby boy. He has been a great joy to all of us and we are all very glad that he came into our lives.

About nine months after our nephew came along, we also applied to New Beginnings. We were so excited when we got our acceptance letter saying that we had been approved and were on the waiting list for our precious baby.

During our waiting time, we prepared our hearts, home and lives for the arrival of our baby. We were very excited and were anxiously awaiting the call from New Beginnings telling us we were parents.

Fourteen months after receiving our acceptance letter, we received The Call from Debbie Velie telling us we have a baby girl. We rushed around and left quickly to go see our baby girl. We were both very thrilled and excited.

Throughout the whole long process, New Beginnings was wonderful. The staff took the time to answer my questions and make the things easier.

Our family owes a lot to New Beginnings and the birthmothers they care for. If not for New Beginnings and brave birth parents our family wouldn't have our baby girl or our precious nephew.

A Girl Named Melly
Melody and Vicki Jensen

My name is Melody but everyone calls me Melly. And this is my story.

Many years ago my Mommy and Daddy decided they wanted a baby girl to love. After years of prayers and dreams I arrived quite unexpectedly on Thanksgiving Day 2003!

Just as Mommy, Daddy and Nana were sitting down to Thanksgiving dinner, the phone rang. Everyone thought it was Daddy's parents calling to say "Happy Thanksgiving!"

Boy was Mommy surprised when the call was from the adoption agency. After Mommy's initial shock, she told Daddy to pick up another phone and listen. Mommy and Daddy then listened to Miss Debbie Velie say that I had been born and they were going to be my parents.

While Mommy and Daddy were talking to Miss Debbie, Nana asked whose baby they were discussing. When Mommy pointed to herself and Daddy, Nana nearly fainted. She had to hold onto the counter to stand up.

Mommy and Daddy told Miss Debbie they'd call her back soon and let her know what time they'd pick me up. Everyone was shell shocked after the phone call. Mommy, Daddy and Nana sat down, made plans to pick me up and tried to eat. Mommy was too nervous and excited to eat so she made lists of everything that needed to be done and everyone that needed to be called.

65

Mommy and Daddy called Miss Debbie to let her know they were ready to leave and would be at her house in about four hours.

Daddy drove since Mommy was too nervous. During the four hour drive, Mommy made lots of phone calls to tell my family and friends all about me.

Some people were difficult to find but by the time Mommy and Daddy picked me up, my whole family knew I had arrived.

Everyone was very excited and shocked about my arrival. No one was expecting The Call to come on Thanksgiving Day!

When Mommy and Daddy got to Miss Debbie's house, I was wrapped in a towel after just having a bath. I was three days old and very small. Mommy and Daddy were almost scared to pick me up because I was so small. I barely weighed five pounds and looked very fragile.

Mommy and Daddy both say that when Miss Debbie put me in Mommy's arms for the first time it was love at first sight. I couldn't imagine anyone else being my parents and Mommy and Daddy couldn't imagine any other baby as theirs.

We spent the first night as a family at Nana's house. The next day we went home. I met my Great Grandma Mimi on my way home. She loved me at first sight. I was very excited to be home and meet my family.

My Nana, Aunt Jennifer, Uncle Michael, and Cousin Sam were waiting for me when I got home. Izzy B, my new dog, sniffed me to see if I was OK to stay. I love Izzy B and she loves me.

66

Over the next few months, I met more family and friends. I get lots of attention and I love every minute of it. I love being Melly and I love my parents.

I am proof that God answers prayers. We give thanks every day that my birthmother had the courage to place me with Mommy and Daddy!

And so this story ends, but my life is just beginning!

Rhea's Discovery
Rhea Palmer

My curiosity as to what my natural mother looks like dates back to when I was around three.

Mom and I were watching a Sonny and Cher show and Mom tells me that I asked, "Is that what my mother looks like?"

Mom said yes and so began the fantasy every adopted child has of having famous parents.

As I grew older, and reality set in, I resigned myself to the fact that my birthparents were normal people (although, I did allow myself just a fantasy or two!).

My adoptive parents were always frank with me about how I came to them.

My birth-grandmother, Virginia O'Kelly, was dating a man who worked in a steel mill with my Dad. This man was the one who told my adoptive parents about me.

The adoption went smoothly and I was moved into my new home in Memphis, Tennessee.

Mom did withhold all names until I was around twelve or thirteen.

My birth certificate was incorrect, but it was mentioned that it would probably be better to just leave it the way it was in case I got a wild hair at a later point and wanted to search for my birth family.

That was also when I found out that I wasn't born in Meridian, Mississippi but rather Oxford, Mississippi. I liked the idea of Oxford better. No offense to fellow Meridianites, but the idea of being an Ole Miss Rebel had more appeal to a pre-teen.

A few years later, Mom and I tried making a few phone calls to track down the whereabouts of Carol O'Kelly. We knew she married someone with the last name of Hillhouse and we had a general idea of where she lived at the time. We started calling and pretty much came to a dead end. I wasn't computer-literate at the time so the Internet wasn't an option for me.

A few years after that, I started getting the fever again. By this time, I was well acquainted with the Internet and started to poke around again—this time looking in places such as: www.adoption.com and www.ancestry.com.

Every time I would come up empty-handed. Carol was no where to be found. Her mother Virginia, was no where to be found either. I had no current last names, no history past 1973. I was discouraged and gave up the search.

One night I started looking again, just on a whim. I was pretty skeptical by this time and wasn't really expecting much out of this search. I was a dog with a bone, though. I had to try again.

I tried using just the search engine to find them instead of going through websites as I had done in the past.

I typed in Carol O'Kelly. Nothing.

Then I typed in Virginia O'Kelly. A few lines down I came across "RRN Family."

The mention of Mississippi caught my eye, and I saw the name Virginia Crouch O'Kelly Bratton. I clicked the link and found the family tree attached to Wayne and Barbara Carter's Ridge Rider News website.

Still skeptical, I browsed through the names, clueless as to who they were. Then I scanned Virginia's children. There she was: Carol O'Kelly Mullins.

This was too good to be true. I'll admit I was still skeptical even though it was right in front of me. At 10:30 that night I called Mom. She's a night owl and is used to me calling about goofy stuff!

Over the next hour and a half we managed to convince ourselves I hit the jackpot.

I decided to send an e-mail to the main address and see what came out of it.

I wasn't thinking of the consequences, which I feel I ought to explain at this point. Never in all my searching had I planned to just contact my natural mother out-of-the-blue. I had no idea what I would be walking into. I had it in my head that depending on the situation, I would send a letter.

For all I knew, she had a new life and family who did not have knowledge of me. I never felt I was lacking anything because of my adoption, but the curiosity was there.

I felt comfortable sending this particular e-mail, though, because this wasn't a direct relative. To avoid conflict, I mentioned for genealogical reasons I was interested in a couple of people listed on their family tree. I sent the e-mail before I had a chance to

70

change my mind and spent a sleepless night wondering what sort of response I would get.

I had so much going on inside my head. There were emotions I didn't even realize I had.

I had gone into my initial search for my mother with the idea I wanted family tree information or medical history.

I was an O'Kelly with red hair. I figured I had some kind of Irish background somewhere. I had no medical background. What if I needed it?

Nothing prepared me for what I felt after sending that e-mail. All of a sudden, I WANTED it to be the right family. I WANTED to know what Carol looked like. Did she look like me? Mom had mentioned I was physically like Virginia. I wanted to see pictures of her to see if it was true.

The next morning, on Mother's Day, I received an e-mail back from Wayne telling me that I had the right people.

After giving me some additional information, he wrote, "This is not a requirement for us helping you, but we are curious as to what your interest is since we cannot find any mention of you anywhere."

Well, I was floored. I mean, **floored**! I remember sitting there just kind of staring dumbly at the e-mail I had just received, wondering what in the world was I going to do now. This was the moment I had been waiting for and I had no idea what to do with it.

It's always amazing when we read something that we find hard to comprehend we re-read it time and time again thinking the words will somehow just go poof and disappear or read something like, "Ha, Ha, fooled you!" Well, Uncle Wayne, your words did not disappear and I was still sitting there reading them over and over again. Just in case.

Trying to sound impartial and perky, I wrote back saying something like, "Thank you. That was what I was looking for. I don't blame you for being curious, because I do have additional information about them. May I contact you by phone?"

Now I was really on pins and needles. Everything I had ever heard about adopted children meeting their natural parents came rushing back to me.

I was expecting anything from a wonderful reunion to a hostile response saying I needed to stay out of Caryl's life.

I had psyched myself up for the worst and still nearly dropped the phone when I saw the call come in.

It was Barbara.

I was so nervous I don't recall details of what we talked about. I do remember the feelings, though.

And it was wonderful, absolutely wonderful.

All of a sudden, nothing else mattered but the fact I was in contact with my natural great-aunt and uncle. Everything was okay now. We talked and talked and talked. How in the world do you catch up on 30 years of everything in an hour and a half?

We set up a meeting for that next Saturday. That gave me a week to plan my questions and gather my pictures.

Saturday morning I was ready. I shut everything out on the drive down except for my radio. I knew if I allowed myself to think I would be a nervous wreck by the time I made it to Pontotoc.

So I wasn't prepared for the reception I got. Uncle Wayne and Aunt Barbara seemed overjoyed to see me. I couldn't believe it. When Barbara hugged me, it was the first time I felt myself lose control and tear up. Yes, Uncle Wayne, hugs like that are reserved for special occasions!

That whole day was the shortest day of my life. We laughed and talked and caught up on everything. All the gaps were filled in that day. It was neat to listen to them mention my resemblance to Cheryl, Carol, and Brigitte.

I had always heard people say I looked like my adoptive Mom and Dad, but I had always chalked it up to them saying what they thought I wanted to hear. This was a REAL resemblance.

We looked through more pictures than I could count. Tons of them. I was still in shock at the reception I received. I was still in shock that I was even there. My brain was in overdrive trying to remember the names and faces and dates and events of the family I never knew.

It is impossible to write in a short space everything I went through that day. I left to go home that night at 11:00, still not really ready to leave. I have had a wonderful life with my adoptive parents and I wouldn't change it for the world, but I am also blessed with an extended family now. And that I wouldn't change for the world either!

73

Grandparents Times Two!
Michael and Jennifer Johnson

My adoption story is not your typical adoption story. I don't have any adopted children myself, but I am the grandparent of two beautiful and amazing adopted children. I'd like to share with you how adoption and New Beginnings changed my life forever.

Just over two and a half years ago my life was forever changed by a single phone call. That miraculous call came from my youngest daughter. She called to tell me that she had just become a Mommy!

You see, her life had also been changed in an instant by a phone call. That call came from New Beginnings letting her and her husband know that their years of prayers and waiting had been answered. They were the proud new parents of a baby boy.

My daughter, Jennifer, and her husband, Michael, had tried for several years to have a baby but were never able to.

When they decided to adopt they were told it could take anywhere from three to five years before an infant became available. Much to our astonishment, however, they received the call only six months after being approved to adopt!

Our hearts were certainly ready for this precious boy's arrival, but we had to kick into overdrive to get everything ready for his homecoming. Of course we didn't complain one bit.

We welcomed Samuel, the newest member of our family with open hearts and open arms. Samuel means "God heard" and God had certainly heard our prayers for a child.

What a delight it was to hold my grandson in my arms for the first time and know that my daughter's years of waiting and aching for a child were over.

My family's story does not end there, though. About a year and a half later New Beginnings called our family again. This call was to my eldest daughter and her husband on Thanksgiving Day.

They became the proud new parents of a baby girl. As the turkey grew cold and the dressing congealed we hastily prepared for another miracle baby! Vicki, my daughter, and David, her husband, drove to Tupelo that afternoon to meet their daughter.

There are no words to describe the joy and love they held in their hearts for her long before they ever laid eyes on her. Melody became part of our family that day and what a joy she has been. That is a Thanksgiving we will never forget. We truly had something to be thankful for that day.

It has been such a beautiful blessing to see my two grandchildren grow and play together. Sam, my grandson, is now three years old. He has the most amusing sense of humor and is incredibly resourceful. He keeps us rolling in laughter. My son-in-law has a similar sense of humor so I can see where Sam gets his! He loves to sing and dance and he enjoys books and playing outside.

Melody, my granddaughter, is eighteen months old now. Like her name, her laughter is a melody to our ears. She is our monkey. She climbs over everything. Her mother did the same

75

things as a child! I think we may have a future gymnast on our hands.

Because of new Beginnings and the miracle of adoption my family is complete. Both of my daughters who thought they might never be mothers now have beautiful children to hold. Their arms are no longer empty and our family is truly blessed by these two miracles. There are no words to completely express my thanks and gratitude to the women who loved these children enough to give them up, They are very special to me and I will always remember them in my prayers.

I am incredibly thankful for New Beginnings and the ministry they provide. They are certainly a place of new beginnings. Who knows, maybe we have more new beginnings in our future. I would love to hear the sound of even more laughter in our family.

Grandma and the Grandchildren
Eunice Velie

In September of 1982, Bill and I were privileged to become grandparents to Corinne Renee when she arrived from Korea.

She was our firstborn grandchild, but we didn't meet her until she was six months old. But that didn't matter - she was beautiful! In May 1984 we were blessed again when Shaina Lynn arrived from Korea. These two precious girls have been a special part of the fabric of our family ever since.

Over the years, I have spent many hours with the girls. They lived in our city for a few years, and I could easily go get them and bring them to our home, or I could visit them at their home. We did many things together such as going to church, to parks, spending time with their cousins, riding on rides at the mall, and spending nights at Grandma's.

They were missed by all when they moved to Mississippi.

Well, I thought it was necessary for Cori and Shaina, and the rest of my grandchildren, to still be with Grandma. So, I would travel from Wisconsin to Mississippi to take care of them and our other grandchildren who had also moved to Mississippi. I would spend about six weeks out of the summer there.

As they grew a little older, I thought they needed to come to Grandma's house, so I would go pick them up and bring them to Wisconsin for about six weeks.

About seven years ago Corinne and I spent a month in Korea as a guest of E.J. Kim, a missionary to South Korea. Our trip was a life-changing experience and we both came home appreciating the work of foreign missionaries and our home - the country of America.

Corrine is now married to a wonderful husband and is a mother of a handsome little son, Ethan, my great-grandson. Shaina is now part of the work force at a department store. We are proud of our beautiful granddaughters!

If you, or other members of your family, are thinking of adopting internationally, please do so. You will be a blessing and **you** will be blessed.

Twice The Blessing
Randy, Dana, Miranda, Reece and Riley Bittel

When my husband and I decided we would try to have children, little did we know that the turn of events would lead us to adopting identical twin boys less than a year later.

After trying several different procedures, with the failure of pregnancy, we decided to look into adoption.

I had always felt in my heart that I would adopt a child or children. I guess you could say it was God preparing me for what He had for us.

We started looking into international adoption as many couples do now days. The cost would be higher, but the wait would be shorter and there are so many countries to look at. There were so many options and avenues we could take with international adoption.

At first, we signed up with an agency and starting looking at the country Ukraine. The adoptions in Ukraine had been put on hold, so we started looking at Russia or Guatemala. During this time, my husband and I decided to try in-vitro, which too was a failure. I was totally devastated when my pregnancy test came back negative.

I felt like I was at my wits end. I started asking God if I was ever going to have children. I asked God to take away the desire to have children if I wasn't going to be blessed with any. I was sad, mad and angry at God for not blessing me with children. I had all but given up.

But, I thought I would try one more avenue which led me to New Beginnings.

I dropped off my paperwork and talked to DebbieVelie. I could tell that New Beginnings would help us if at all possible.

Four weeks after dropping off our paperwork, we got the call. Yes, the call that would change our lives forever.

We tried not to get to excited but you can't help yourself. We talked on the way to the agency about everything from baby names - to could we afford twins if this was really true? Yes, you heard me right**....twins!**

This was a double blessing. Could God really be moving in our favor with this birthmother? I believe the birthmother looked at other couples, but we were the ones that she had chosen and this was to be an open-adoption. She still had another six weeks before her due date and it would seem like forever.

This included doctor appointments with sonograms, getting to know the birthmom and her family and much more.

When the day arrived for the twins to be born I was excited, but scared. I actually got to enter labor and delivery to see the birth of my beautiful twin boys. They were the prettiest babies I had ever seen.

Every Mississippi birthmother must wait 72 hours before being allowed to surrender her parental rights. This would be the longest 72 hours of our life. Finally, the day came and went without a glitch in the plan: God had shown His mercy and grace upon our lives once again.

Through all this we learned that it's not our plan that needs to be concentrated on, it's God's plan. As His children it's sometimes hard to comprehend and to be patient with His master plan. So be faithful in the little and maybe God will bless you with a double portion as He did us.

A Grave Decision

We have chosen to include a few testimonies that were written pertaining to abortion.

These true stories offer forgiveness, healing and understanding.

Abortion is an option that is allowed by law in America.

On the average business day in American there are over 5,000 unborn children aborted.

Statistics tell us that almost 1.2 million children are aborted, while 1.2 million adoptive couples wait each year.

I know Mike and Maria in the following story. If they had known what adoption offered, they would have chosen adoption.

In this great nation of ours, isn't it time that we offered more life and hope to hurting, frightened birthmothers and birthfathers. Abortion isn't always the easy way out and we pray that you will "choose life" if you are reading this book and seeking an answer to your dilemma. Adoption is the better choice. – Tom Velie

From the Heart of a Father
Michael Bysina

To me, the interesting thing about the overwhelming majority of stories involving abortion is that they tend to focus on the birthmother or the unborn child. Those are the true and only victims of abortion, right?

What some may not realize is that the effects of this tragic decision - I often think of it as a crime - also impacts the emotional and mental state of the birthfather.

While I would agree that, in most cases, the woman suffers the greater psychological trauma of the incident, mine included, in some cases a man can be traumatized and mentally affected just as much.

While I was a junior in high school, I went through one of the scariest scenarios in my life at the time. I made the foolish mistake of getting my girlfriend pregnant.

The idea of having to approach my parents about this was absolutely torturous. Quite honestly, at the time of the incident, I was more concerned about the punishment and shame I would endure. I wasn't very concerned about the "non-living thing called a fetus."

My parents, along with my girlfriend's mother, determined that having an abortion was the only alternative for us. At such a young age, I guess I also thought that this would be the easy way out. Or, so I thought.

83

Well, "I" made it through the ordeal (it was all about me wasn't it) and survived the punishment that my parents imposed at the time. And quite frankly, it did not really bother me that much for several years. Simply because during those years, I was like any teenager – immature.

Nonetheless, it seemed as I grew older, especially beginning in my early twenties, that I remember having to deal with the inner turmoil of knowing that I was, at least partially, responsible for the death of a baby.

The older I became, the tougher this was to deal with.

It's not that it affected my everyday life in terms of functioning normally, but some days, behind closed doors – and as I lay to sleep at night – I would think about it deeply.

I came to the point of tears and wrestled with this inescapable burden that was tugging at my very soul.

The ultimate question for me was, how could I have been so selfish? And, was God ever going to forgive me for my decision?

When I reached the age of 28, I found my way to a Pentecostal altar where I discovered that I was able to place the hidden sins of my soul onto the shoulders of my Savior, Jesus Christ.

True repentance, at the feet of the only true God, was the cure for this burden that was graciously and mercifully lifted by the blood of the Lamb. Praise God!!!

Although this act will never totally leave my mind, in terms of simply knowing what happened, I am instantly comforted each and every time in knowing that God has forgiven and forgotten this sin.

I believe that any man who allows a child to die before birth, and who has a living conscience, will be perpetually tormented by his actions unless he seeks the forgiving open arms of Jesus.

Consequences
Maria Yakos

Deuteronomy 30:19,20
This day I call heaven and earth as witnesses against you that I have set before you life and death, blessings and curses. Now choose life, so that you and your children may live and that you may love the Lord your God; listen to his voice and hold fast to him.

Every day people make choices. Often they are bad choices with dire consequences.

How can we, when we have the ability to help, make any other choice but to help them?

According to statistics from Focus on the Family, 44% of all American women will have an abortion at some point in their lifetime.

It has been said, "A woman chooses abortion like an animal caught in a trap chooses to gnaw off its leg."

In 1981, I chose abortion as a way out of a crisis pregnancy. At the time, I felt trapped and like there was no other option.

Today, women across our nation will make that same decision.

Most of these women will not hear about alternatives to abortion.

There is a better way and there is a way we can help.

86

First, parents - as God's appointed authority - have a tremendous opportunity to educate and prepare their children. A child will remember their parents' words and actions when faced with urgent decisions; the home needs to be a place of safety and support.

Secondly, we need to promote the other options available.

Adoption is a choice everyone can live with.

Crisis pregnancy centers and homes for unwed mothers are struggling in the fight to save lives and spare women the devastation of an abortion experience. They need our assistance.

We must realize that abortion has touched every level of society. It is not someone else's problem.

Lastly, most people are unaware of the trauma that a woman faces after her abortion experience.

Many women who choose abortion are going against their own moral code.

In a survey on 260 post abortive women, over 50% of the women responded they agreed their decision to abort was "inconsistent with her prior beliefs and a betrayal of her own ideals."

In *Forbidden Grief*, by **Theresa Burke**; she writes:

Consequently, many women experience trauma known as Post Abortion Syndrome. The inability to process the guilt, anger, and grief related to the abortion will bring symptoms such as: depression, suicidal thoughts, flashback memories, nightmares, eating disorders, etc. The truth about the painful consequences of abortion is not common knowledge in our country. Since there is so much pain, women bear the consequences in secrecy.

87

Breaking the silence about abortion and its consequences will help those facing a crisis pregnancy to choose life and live.

It also will help to bring healing to those who have carried the awful secret and pain of their abortion choice.

There are words of life that will bring blessing and not cursing. We can help others to choose life and live.

RESOURCES:

Focus on the Family - *Healing After Abortion* by Teri Ki Reisser, M.S.,M.F.T. and Paul C. Reisser, M.D.Copyright – 2002
Forbidden Grief by Theresa Burke with David C. Reardon Copyright 2002; Published by Acorn Books - Springfield Illinois

If God Heard the Voice of Abel's Blood...
What is He Hearing Now?
Tom Velie

When the tragically fatal tsunami struck Southeast Asia in December 2004, humanity responded in an unprecedented way. Fingers were pointed by world leaders, vociferously accusing the other of failing to "give enough." Within six months, the finger-pointing stopped as billions of dollars in cash and aid poured into the stricken areas.

The death toll counters rolled forward each day and we saw the number rise from 20,000 to 50,000, to 100,000, with some of the final estimates being in the 150,000 range. Yes, 150,000 lives lost within a few moments of time. Of those swept to sea, only a handful survived. Two former U.S. Presidents continue to appeal for aid, church organizations tally the giving on their web pages, and billboards encourage us to give more through world humanitarian organizations.

And yet..."very few ever hear the cry of the other 150,000." I pondered that thought during a cross-country flight to visit a family elder.

Did God know the final impact of the tsunami's driving force? "Of course He did," I thought, and then my mind staggered as the realization of God's infinite knowledge, sensitivity and compassion overwhelmed me.

"I heard Abel's blood." That one response pierced my mind, as my eyes scanned the earth's unending horizon while flying over

89

it at 35,000 feet. And so…if God heard Abel's blood, what is He hearing now?

God's Word records the pain-filled utterance following the rage-driven murder of one, innocent, righteous man: *"And He (God) said, "What hast thou done? The voice of thy brother's blood crieth unto me from the ground." (Genesis 4:10, KJV).*

And yet, with the blood of 46 million aborted voices, crying from the earth, in America alone, are we hearing the cry? Is it possible that our hearts are dulled and insensitive, while this earthen globe reels and shudders with natural disaster after natural disaster in response to the cacophony of voices?

Perhaps the earth groans *(Romans 8:22)*, while we ignore the voices of 150,000 babies (a number equal to the tsunami victims) who are aborted every 32 business days in America.

"I'm glad that New Beginnings is concerned about pregnant girls and their unborn babies - we're just too busy to get involved with that issue," were the piercing words spoken to us recently from one church leader.

Yes, we always listen to the frightened, confused teenagers (your daughters, your sons and your youth) who call us wondering where to turn to for compassionate counsel. They're pleading for someone to listen as they fearfully face their, seemingly, hopeless dilemma.

And, unbelievably, we sometimes hear that they receive counsel, by "so-called" spirit-filled pastoral staff, to consider abortion as a solution to an unplanned pregnancy. Perhaps if we will listen we will hear. I believe that God hears the "voices" and the cry is deafening…do you hear it?

Forgiveness 70 times 70
Maria Yakos

II Corinthians 1:3-4, KJV
Blessed be God, even the Father of our Lord Jesus Christ, the
Father of mercies, and the God of all comfort; Who comforteth
us in all our tribulation, that we may be able to comfort them
which are in any trouble, by the comfort wherewith we ourselves
are comforted of God.

Life gives everyone of us our own tough times.

It is good to have someone who has been there who can say,
"God is able, even in this, to bring good."

As I look back on the darkest days of my life, I can see how God
spoke words of hope and healing through the man who would
later become my husband.

In April of my sophomore year of college, I made the decision to
have an abortion. When the doctor informed me that I was
pregnant and asked me what are I was going to do, I did not think
there was any other decision for me but to terminate the
pregnancy.

It was not the "easy" answer and I soon found out that it was a
decision that brought grave consequences. The physical and
emotional damage I experienced could only be healed by the
touch of God's grace, and I can see now that God, in His mercy,
immediately began to reach for me.

91

God's grace is truly amazing. It is immediate forgiveness. When Jesus said to forgive seventy times seventy, it was because He is a God who is willing to forgive us.

The story of Adam and Eve and the first sin demonstrates God's forgiveness. It is amazing that by the evening of the day Adam and Eve sinned, God was already giving them a promise of a Messiah. In Genesis 3:15, God gives Adam and Eve hope for a future Saviour. The Bible calls Him "the lamb slain from the foundation of the world." It was in His plan to touch mankind with his forgiveness and bring healing to every consequence of sin.

Is it surprising then, that God would place people in our lives who could speak words of life to us.

I met Brad the month after my abortion. When I realized that he was serious about our relationship and that I was falling in love, I knew that I wanted to tell him about my abortion. I was scared and did not know how he would respond, but I did not want to keep such a major part of my life from him.

The words he spoke the night I talked with him will forever be a message of God's love and mercy. "I am not worried about your past, what I want is your future."

That is the powerful message of the love and mercy of God. He does not see the sinner, He sees the future He wants for us. As we allow God, he heals spiritually, emotionally and physically. His touch is complete because the work of Calvary is complete.

There are some trials that we have to go alone. The road is lonely and we lean on a God we cannot see and sometimes cannot feel. However, there is healing, there is a future, and there is hope.

If You Ever Want A Son, I'm Available
Stephen M. Drury
Co-Founder and Chairman, NBICFS

Having been a minister for over thirty years, I enjoy watching the faces as I tell the audience that our son was born ten days before my wife and I got married. Normally, there are quite a few seconds when the entire congregation is silent, as if they can't believe a preacher would admit from the pulpit to such a shameful folly in his life prior to marriage.

But it is true.

Our son was born December 7, 1972 and Evelyn and I were married December 17, 1972. The first time we "knew" about our son happened rather uniquely.

I wanted my pastor, Nathanial A. Urshan to dedicate our second baby daughter, Mendy Christine. As we stood in front of the pulpit at Calvary Tabernacle in Indianapolis, Indiana for her dedication, a very strange event took place.

At one point in the dedication ceremony, Pastor Urshan stated that Mendy was our third child. Since Mendy was our second child, not third, we caught his attention and mentioned publicly that she was our second child, not third. He was quick to say it wasn't true, she was our third child ... and added that it was a prophetic statement.

Of course we laughed ... Pastor Urshan just didn't like to be wrong was our thinking. But he was so emphatic ... and now we know he was right.

93

Mendy was our third child. We had another one born ten days before we were married. We just hadn't met him yet.

James came to the children's home, where I served as President for 23 years, when he was twelve years of age. When he was fourteen, two memorable events melted our hearts toward him.

The first was during an annual Church conference in St. Louis, Missouri in 1986. We always tried take one or two of the home's young people with us to help pass out our grant materials various departments. Of course, we always mentioned to them what a difference these ministries had made by provided housing and other needs for the children who were with us.

One evening during the conference, Evelyn and I had a late event to attend. We had ordered pizzas to be delivered to the room for our two daughters and James. When we returned that night to the motel room, all three were asleep. Stephenie and Mendy were under the covers and James had fallen asleep at the end of the bed by the girl's feet. As we walked in the room, we were touched by the need of this handsome young man and how well he got along with our daughters. It was such a warm scene … it looked like they belonged together.

A few weeks later, another event took place. Orthodontists in Tupelo, MS would do free work for the children who most needed work on their teeth. James was one of the young people who were blessed to receive these free services. For some reason, his housemother was not available one day to pick him up from the dentist, so my wife "volunteered." Looking back, I wonder about her "spirit of volunteerism".

We were building a new home at the time so she told James that she was going to go by the new property on the return trip. While at the construction site, she explained what each room was going to have in it. We constantly had guests in our home and our girls often had to sleep on the floor or on the couch in our living room. The new home was to have separate bedrooms and a guest room. When my wife showed the room to James, that was to be the guest room, he said, "Oh, you mean my room."

The next Sunday at church, James came to my wife, put his arm around her shoulder and said, "If you ever decide you need a son, I'm available!"

When we moved into our new home, guess who moved in with us? James. We didn't have a guest room until he went away to college.

As I recently sat through my former pastor's funeral in Indianapolis, I reflected on the many times and ways Pastor Urshan affected our lives individually and as a family. I didn't understand his words during Mendy's dedication, but he was right. She was our third child. We just hadn't met the one born ten days before we were married.

Our family became complete when James became our son through adoption. We are so very thankful and proud of him. We can't imagine our family without him. It's like he was there ... even at our wedding.

What Could Have Been...And Is Not
Kristen Butler

I was adopted by a young Apostolic couple when I was only three days old.

Phil and Paula were married in July of 1974 at the young and tender ages of 21 and 20, respectively.

They both knew that they wanted children and not too long after they were married, they decided it was time to begin their family.

Sadly, and much to their disappointment, Paula was diagnosed with endometriosis and was told that she may never be able to have children.

For nine long years they tried to start a family. Every attempt was made and there was no option that would be ruled out. They had placed themselves on several adoption waiting lists and Paula had undergone infertility treatments.

They bought baby furniture and baby clothes, all the equipment and goodies that a baby needs, furniture for an older child, they had even picked out baby names for a boy and a girl. Everything was ready; all they needed was a baby.

That is where I came in...I'm their, now-grown, "baby."

Because of adoption, I had the opportunity to be raised as a Christian in an Apostolic home. My grandfather was my pastor, I was involved in every activity that a young person could possibly be involved in, I was enrolling in Bible college, and yet

I always felt cheated because I didn't know my background, where I had "come from" or my bloodline.
So I searched...

Finally, when I was 17, I met my birth family. As soon as I met them, I wanted to fall on my knees and praise God for what He had kept me from by allowing me to be adopted, not only into a stable and loving family, but also into His family!

I found out that God had His protective hand on me even before I was born.

I was the illegitimate child of an 18-year-old girl whose husband was in the service and had been out to sea for some time. When she found out that she was pregnant for the second time, (I have an older brother who was also placed for adoption), she told my birthfather (not her husband) and his reply was that he knew where she could go to have an abortion.

Thankfully, her conscience kept her from going along with his idea!

All throughout her pregnancy she smoked and drank. A month after her husband returned from his military duties, she was four months pregnant, but she was ashamed of her unfaithfulness and told him she was only one month pregnant and that the baby was his. Her husband was overjoyed! He loved kids and had always wanted to be a father.

When my birthmother went into labor, everyone thought that I would be three months premature, because her husband hadn't been home long enough for it to be a full-term pregnancy. She was rushed to the Indiana University Medical Center where everyone was anticipating an underweight, premature baby.

97

Much to the surprise of the doctors, and her husband, I was born weighing just shy of nine pounds.

My birthmother's husband loved me like I was his own - because for six months during the pregnancy, he thought that I was his child. But he didn't feel that at his young age he would have the mental strength to raise a child that was not legitimately his.

Putting me up for adoption was the mutual decision of two young kids who wanted me to have a better life.

Some birthmothers and birthfathers don't have the selflessness to realize that their child would have a better life, filled with more opportunities with another couple. I was one of the lucky ones.

Three months after I was born and put up for adoption, her husband filed for divorce and later she remarried. Had she decided to keep me, I would have been the stepchild to her violently abusive second husband.

Don't get me wrong, I love my biological family very much and I continue to be very close to them, but I don't think I have to point out the obvious miracles that God had already performed before I had even been released from the hospital.

Now 22 years later, my life still isn't perfect, but through all of my trials I knew that if it weren't for the amazing parents that God provided me with, my life would be in shambles. God has brought me through a lot of problems, most of which I got myself into, that I would have never been able to find a way out of on my own.

I may not have everything I want, but He has given me everything I need.

Shopping For Kristen
Paula and Phil Butler – Kristen's Parents

On January 3rd, 1983, Paula dragged her husband to the mall to make Christmas returns and to hit the after-Christmas sales. Paula was, and continues to be, a talented sale shopper.

Phil didn't want to be there, and would have rather been at home watching a football game, but he decided to amuse his wife, earn some points and to tag along.

"I need to go to Lazarus and Penney's, is there any place in particular that you want or need to go?" Paula implored of her husband.

In all honesty, Phil just wanted to go to the nearest bookstore and lose himself in the shelves of the season's best sellers and forego the whole busy after-Christmas shopping/returning fiasco.

"Not really, I just need to call the office to check my messages. But I'll meet you at Penney's in an hour," he replied, pointing at a nearby kiosk of payphones.

Paula headed off to do her returns as Phil, happy that he escaped having to navigate his way through the crowds, walked over to the payphones. Phil spoke with his secretary for a few moments before asking about his messages and tried to find a pen to write them down.

The first message caught his attention immediately. "Phil, you received a call from the Suemma-Coleman adoption agency. It's very important that you return this call as soon as possible."

Trying to keep his excitement and hopes down to a responsible level, Phil wrote down the number and proceeded to return the call.

Could this be the call that he and Paula had been praying for? After seven long years of wanting a child, was God about to answer their prayers?

"Phil, we have a baby girl for you," the social worker said. "She is three days old and we just brought her here to the agency. It's okay if you can't pick her up by four o'clock this afternoon, she will simply be placed in a foster home for the night and you and Paula can pick her up tomorrow."

Phil was speechless. He didn't know what to say. They were finally going to be parents! "No we'll pick her up this afternoon," he said once he found his voice and gathered his thoughts. "We'll be there in…" He looked at his watch. It was three o'clock and the agency was across town. But there was plenty of time if they left the mall right away. "…How about thirty minutes?" he asked.

"Phil, you know that all you're getting is a baby, right?" asked the social worker. **Only a baby?!?!?** Was she crazy? A baby was all they ever wanted.

"Yes, Pam, that's all we want," he replied.

"No," she said. "There are no diapers, no blankets, bottles, formula. We can't send the baby home with you unless you have these things."

Phil's mind raced. All of those things had already been bought, but they were of course at home, not in the trunk of the car.

He and Paula had to go buy all of these things and get to the other side of Indianapolis in an hour.

He thanked the caseworker, told her that they would be there by four o'clock and hung up the phone. He stretched his full six-foot-three-inch frame to see over the heads of the post-holiday shoppers in an attempt to spot his wife. Finally he spotted her.

He started screaming for her. "Paula!" He jumped up and down and waved his arms in the air to get her attention. He was oblivious to the odd stares that were being shot his way by the other mall shoppers.

Paula turned and spotted her husband. Frantically she ran to him, terrified that something was wrong.

"We have our baby!!" he exclaimed to his out-of-breath wife.

Shock, amazement, joy and a million other emotions flooded Paula's heart. After hearing what the caseworker had told Phil, she hurriedly began fishing change out of her purse. Tying up three of the six payphones at the kiosk, the two called their parents and Paula's siblings.

Amid switching phones and getting tangled up in the cords, Phil remembered that they were on a very tight time schedule. He turned to Paula and told her that they only had 45 minutes to buy all of the supplies and get to the agency or they would have to wait to be united with their precious little girl until the next day.

Phil went to the drugstore for bottles and formula, not having the first clue how to pick out the right stuff. Paula ran to the nearest baby-clothing store to get blankets and other necessities. By the time the excited couple got to the car and on their way, they only had 30 minutes left. Running every red light, miraculously avoiding any accidents or watchful policemen, they raced to the adoption agency.

At precisely four o'clock, Paula and Phil were running up the stairs of Suemma-Coleman adoption agency, taking the stairs two at a time. Armed with their purchases, the couple burst through the caseworker's door.

There in that very room laid the most beautiful baby girl that they had ever seen.

After signing the necessary paperwork, they finally had their baby girl. Kristen DeAnn lay sleeping in her new parent's arms.

Love Is Obvious
April Bruce-Stewart, Granddad's Daughter

My dad has just been diagnosed, estimated at 99% accuracy, with Alzheimer's Disease.

One of the symptoms he's exhibiting is technically called, "poor mood lability."

When I looked up lability in the dictionary it translates roughly to 'unstable.'

That's an interesting choice of words. I would describe him as also having worn his heart on his sleeve. It's more out there than usual, but there are things to be cherished about people who are who they are, and who don't live behind a facade. But, his facade is ... definitely wearing down.

My daughter, Audrey, a fifteen-year-old, went with my parents, brother and I to see the psychologist about Dad's current level of functioning.

Dad is a retired lawyer. He had requested that Audrey be there. It was a request that surprised me, but a flattered Audrey rearranged her finals schedule to drive out of town with me to be there. Dad had handled both Audrey's, and her younger sister Melody's, adoptions into our family.

While we were in the waiting room, Audrey was cold and snuggled up to her Granddad. He put his arm around her and squeezed her close.

He started to talk about the adoption. We were all there in court; my mom, my dad, my husband, his mother and father, and our 'minor girl child,' as the documents referred to her. His eyes teared up talking about it. He broke down. Audrey squeezed in close and I took over the story he'd begun to recall, as he had so many times before - and this time wasn't able to complete.

"Audrey, what Granddad is remembering is when we went to court to finalize your adoption. He's remembering how happy I was..."

Dad chimed in, "The judge, he ...he looked at your mother..."

"The judge asked if I would come up and take the stand. He asked me to bring the baby with me."

My mom added somewhat accusingly, "She wouldn't let anyone else hold you anyway!" She grinned. Audrey grinned.

I said, "I'd waited a long, long time to hold her, I wasn't going to give her up easily. You'd already had four children, this was my first!"

Dad put in again, choking up and watering at the eyes, "The judge shouldn't have done it that way, he was ..." and he broke down again.

"Audrey, the judge had me bring you up and hold you while I was sworn in and sat on the stand. He started to ask if I had come to love you over the past few weeks, but he stopped himself. Judges usually don't stop themselves."

Dad laughed. Dad cried.

"The judge said, 'I was going to ask you if you love her,...but, I looked at your face and I can't even ask you. I can see it in your face!'"

Dad cried some more and squeezed our now 15 year old "minor girl child."

Mom said, "When the judge had asked your daddy, David, if he loved you, David just said, 'Absolutely!'"

Audrey squeezed her Granddad.

Granddad said, "You've made your mother..." and started to cry again, "...so happy."

And I thought, making me happy, has made him happy.

Audrey's Granddad has repeated this story over and over in the past 15 years. He even ordered a court transcript for Audrey's keepsake box.

She's read the transcript and knows this story from it as well.

He has told me that he didn't know about adoption until we adopted our children. He'd been involved in a number of adoptions as an attorney, but he didn't know it was so real.

When we were all called into the psychologist's office. The news was disheartening. A kick in the stomach for all of us.

He may be forgetting things, but he remembers the important things.And, I'm not so sure I mind this "mood lability" thing.

Birthmom, Thank You for Loving Me
Cori Velie-Taylor

I'm just about ready to be discharged from the hospital when the phone rings.

It is the nurse in the well-baby nursery, calling to tell me that my three-day-old baby boy will have to remain in the hospital due to high levels of bilirubin in his blood.

I stop in the nursery to feed him before going home. After his feeding, I leave the nursery with tears streaming down my face.

I'm surprised at the emotion I feel about leaving this small stranger, even though I will be able to visit over the next couple of days until his release. I can't help but think how my birthmother must have felt 22 years ago when she left me at the Holt orphanage.

She would not be able to come back in a couple of days; her goodbye was forever.

Since I was adopted internationally, there are so many unknowns, but there is only one certainty. My mother loved me. She loved me enough to want me to have what she could not give me even if it meant giving me to another family.

Growing up with an adopted family seems odd to say because it sounds like it is somehow different from growing up with a biological family. I have always felt so much love and respect from my adoptive parents. I don't think I could have felt more loved by any biological family member than I have with my adoptive family.

I couldn't act more like my Dad or be closer to my Mom if I were born to them. I think my growing up years can be summed up with one story.

My cousin, who was ten at the time, was sitting at the table where we were all visiting after dinner. A statement was made about when my sister and I were adopted. My cousin's eyes got really big as she exclaimed, "You were adopted?"

Despite the fact that we were the only Koreans in our Caucasian adopted family, she had never known we were adopted. I don't define myself as "being adopted"; it's just a part of who I am, like my olive skin or jet black hair.

I now work in adoption and am surrounded by it everyday. Often birthmothers will ask me, "How do you feel about your birthmother?" I tell them, "I love her and will always be grateful for the wonderful family that she allowed me to have."

Only in the last 18 months since I have become a mother do I realize what a sacrifice she made for me. If I could say one thing to her it would be, "Thank you for loving me so much."

A Birthmother Speaks Truth
Anonymous

To Birthmothers:

The Lord has laid you on my heart to pray for you and with you during this time of your life.

I also would like to share my testimony with you. I hope that my story will bless you and encourage you to hang on and trust in the Lord. If you follow the leading of God's hand, He will never let you down.

I came from a Christian home. Although I always believed that God was real, He wasn't real in my life. I didn't really understand who He was or what He had to do with my life. My faith was based only on the faith of my parents and those around me.

When I started high school I started fighting a lot with my parents. My dad and I hardly spoke a word to each other unless we were yelling. I wanted to fit in at school and I wanted to live my own life, so I made up my mind to do what I wanted to do.

When I was 15, I met a guy at rehearsals for our school drama. He was two years older than me and I thought he was really awesome. We used to talk for hours. I had never seriously dated anyone before and I really cared for him.

My parents found out that we were dating and they told me I couldn't see him anymore – because he was older and they didn't trust him. So I dated him behind their backs.

As soon as he found out that I was lying to my parents, everything changed. There were no boundaries and no rules. When we would go out, all kinds of things would go on. I felt there was nothing I could do to get out of it. I felt trapped. I just wanted a friend and someone to love me, but he wasn't interested in love and friendship.

Three months went by and in February of 1993 I found out that I was pregnant.

On Valentine's Day I told my parents. They were hurt and angry.

A few weeks later my boyfriend called me from my best friend's house and broke up with me. Then he and my best friend started dating.

He told people at school things that weren't true about me and my reputation, along with friends, were gone.

On top of all that, I was sick for most of the pregnancy. I would have to run out of my classes to the bathroom five or six times every single day. I was so stressed out, I just couldn't handle it.

My parents decided in March that I should go away somewhere to live in a maternity home. My dad was so hurt he would just yell at me for hours, and he just couldn't take the stress of me being there anymore.

Finally, in May, I went to a maternity home/adoption agency. I went there with no friends, no support and no hope. I remember just crying for hours because I hated my life so much. I wanted out of it all.

One night was in our chapel by myself just playing the piano and thinking about everything. I was so frustrated that I laid on the floor and cried and then I prayed.

I said, "God is my refuge, my strength, my peace," and other scriptures in Psalms and various places. Soon I realized that even though my life was still the same - I was different. God had given me a peace that I couldn't understand. I just knew that everything was going to be all right.

I started praying about what to do. I didn't know whether to place the baby for adoption or to be a parent. I wanted to make the right decision, but I was torn.

I didn't have anyone to help me with the baby, but I wanted so much to keep her. I was so blessed to have my case workers, house parents and friends at the house. They constantly stood by my side and helped me through those times of making decisions.

By September I was sure that I was supposed to place the baby for adoption. I was allowed to choose the adoptive parents from profiles that told me a little bit about them, but nothing identifying - like their names.

As soon as I read about the first family – I knew they were the right parents. They were children's ministers. The mom stayed home instead of working, they had waited 10 years to have a baby. They were so excited to adopt that they had been decorating the nursery and collecting stuffed animals for that whole time. Everything about them was perfect.

In October, I had a beautiful baby girl. Everything about her was perfect. I spent some time with her in the hospital and I treasure that time with her so much. I just kept praying that God would give me the strength and wisdom that I needed.

One night, I was holding her in my hospital bed and I just looked at her and I thought about how she deserved the life that God had intended for her. I knew that I could give her all the love in the world, but I had nothing else to give her. I also knew that there was a family that would love her as much as I did and that they had waited and prepared things for her for such a long time.

See, she never belonged to me – she belongs to Jesus. He blessed me with her for a short time, but God intended for her to be in her adoptive home. There is a verse in *Jeremiah 29:11* that says, *"For I know the thoughts that I think toward you, saith the Lord, thoughts of peace, and not of evil, to give you an expected end."* *(KJV)*

Another version of the Bible words it a little differently and says that God knows the plans He has for you, plans for a future and a hope. Not only did God have those plans for me, but also for my precious baby girl.

God prepared me to carry her in my body for nine months, but he had prepared the adoptive family's home to care for her and teach her and to give her everything that she needed. I knew that I had to make the right decision.

Two weeks after she was born, I saw her for the last time. I sang to her, prayed for her, kissed her tiny cheek and said goodbye. That day was one of the hardest days of my life. But I knew that I was making the decision that was best for her.

A few weeks after I placed her, I went back to the maternity house for a visit and my case worker called me into her office. She said that she had something to tell me.

The adoptive parents had prayed about what to name the baby and they felt that God wanted them to share the name he had given them with me. They gave her the same name as my maiden name. They had no idea and still to this day, they don't know. But I knew that God had given me an assurance that she was right where she was supposed to be.

December
Anonymous

To my sweet girl:

I hesitate in beginning this letter for fear I may not say what needs to be said – or will not be able to say what I would like to.

I would like to tell you every detail of the last nine month, but there's not enough paper in the world to hold my thoughts, feelings and prayers. Nor are there words in any language to tell you how much and how many ways that I love you.

I discovered you were growing inside of me in April. I began praying for you. I prayed for your health. I prayed that you would always live for Jesus. I prayed that God would keep you from making the same mistakes I have made.

Every day I wondered what you would look like, how big you would be, what color your eyes would be. I would get so excited whenever I felt you flutter – and later – strong punches and kicks.

You got the hiccups every night at about 10:30 or 11 and sometimes during the day if I was lying down.

Sometimes, lying in bed at night, you would kick so hard the bed would shake.

Every day you grew – my love for you grew stronger and deeper.

Right before I went into the hospital, your grandma and I began looking at profiles of possible adoptive parents. We looked at their ages, their hair color, weight, intended family, their jobs, their house and every other detail we thought important. I wanted everything perfect for you. I prayed that you would be in a family that would be strong in their faith, uphold the standards of the Church and diligently teach you the ways of the Lord. God led us to the family you have now and knowing this – leaves me at peace.

I am worried about you and will always be worried, but I also know that God has His hand on you and your family. He will provide for and protect His own. I truly believe that and now, for you, I have more of a reason to cling to that promise.

When I went into the hospital I couldn't believe the day had finally arrived and I would be able to see your face.

I also knew that it was the beginning of the saddest days of my life.

I went into the operating room wanting to tell the doctor, "Wait! I'm not ready for this baby to come yet. Just give me a few more days with her."

Instead, I waited for some sign from someone that you were born. It seemed to take forever.

As I lay there, listening to the nurses and doctor banter back and forth I suddenly heard your cry fill the air. I cannot describe how I felt at that moment, but when, and only when, you have one of your own children, you will know.

You are my little girl – a part of me that I will never truly let go.

The next three and a half days were wonderful. I kept you in my room day and night only letting the nurses briefly take you away for vital signs. Sometimes when the nurse would bring you in you would be squalling and so angry, but when I would pick you up, you'd be find and content to be held in my arms. As long as you were being loved on and kissed by either your grandma or I, nothing else mattered. I have never felt a bond of love so strong and that love will continue to grow even though we are far apart.

For those few days, your grandma and I were able to spend with you, we laughed and we cried and we loved. You don't realize what a miracle worker you are. You are the one who made me realize how important life is and how important it is to live for God. You are the reason I turned away from my life of sin. You also are the one who bridged a gap between my own mother and I, with your innocent cries and dirty diaper.

When your foster parents came to pick you up, I didn't know if I would be able to let you go.

I dressed you in your new sleeper and wrapped your blanket around you, but in my mind you were just going back to the hospital nursery to have your temperature taken. It was when we got to the van and when I placed you in your car seat – I realized you were leaving for good this time.

My throat constricted and I felt as if I couldn't breathe. I think my heart drew up and closed itself off. I watched you ride away that day, but I am looking forward to the day when I am able to watch you ride back to me.

For now, I am not with you in flesh, but I will always be there in your heart and you will always be in mine. It won't be easy – being without you. I will miss you, and my body will crave to hold you, but I will hold onto the faith that one day I will see you again.

I want you to understand that I didn't place you for adoption because I didn't want you. The opposite is true.

I wanted to keep you there with me forever. That way, I would be able to see you grow up and I would be your mommy.

However, I realize that would have been unfair to you in so many ways. You deserve every opportunity to have the best life. I love you so much I am willing to live without you in my life so that you can have the things I am not able to provide for you. Things such as a stead home, a daddy and being so young and unwise myself, I couldn't teach you things that are important.

I am still growing and changing and don't want you to grow up not being able to properly love and trust or grow up being unsure of yourself. I want you to love your mommy and daddy dearly and I would never try or ever think I could take their place. But I want you to know that my door is always open to you. I can't wait to see your face again. So that I might get to know you and be your friend. At that time I will be open and answer any questions you may have with all honesty.

You are now, and will always be, precious to me. I love you.

Forever yours,
Mother

To My Beautiful Son
Mom

I'm writing you this letter so that one day you will understand why you're not with me.

I hope this answers some of your questions and helps you to appreciate my choice instead of resenting me.

I am really young and I have made some really bad mistakes that put me in the position to have to give you up. If I had known that things would turn out this way, I would have done things differently.

But, as you grow older, you will see that it's not hard to make a wrong choice.

People tell you that you're wrong and you won't be satisfied until you find out for yourself. Then you say, "I wish I had listened."

Your sister was seven months old when your grandma took her to raise until I could get back on my feet and before I knew it, I was pregnant again with you.

I was stuck in a really bad spot then because where we lived, there are no jobs except the construction job that I had.

A pregnant woman has no business working in that kind of a job. So I had to quit. I didn't want to hurt you in any way. I thought that was a good choice, but it just made things harder.

I moved in with your grandma. She supported me and your sister until it came time for her to move out of state with her husband to go to a new job.

I couldn't go. I was so close to having you by that time, and I really needed to stay put. They couldn't afford for me to go anyway.

I had no money, no job, no home, no help – no way to take care of me or you.

So, I sent your sister away with your grandma. I stayed behind.

The adoption agency paid for our apartment until I had you. They paid for everything. I had nothing. They're paying for me to go meet your sister and try to start over and get back on my feet.

The only problem is, I can't have you.

You have no idea how much it hurts me to know that I have to let you go. But, I made a promise to you in the hospital when I was holding you so tight. I promised that I will do better.

I will change things. I will get your sister back and one day, I hope you will let me be a part of your life.

I can't replace what's been taken away from you and I won't try to be your mother, but I would at least like to be your friend.

I love you so much, baby.

But if you choose not to be a part of my life again – I understand. I know that you are with good parents and you should thank God for the love they have given you. And for the life that you wouldn't have had with me. They are truly a blessing and I will love them always for giving you what you deserve.

Know that there isn't a day that goes by that I don't think of you and hold on to the feeling I had when I first held you and kissed you. I'll always remember the way you looked at me.

Once again, I can never say enough – that I love you.

Love,
Mom

To My Baby's New Parents
Anonymous

Throughout my whole pregnancy I have prayed for this newborn baby girl and have prayed for the wisdom to know what's best for her.

Early on in my pregnancy, I decided that I would place her for adoption when she was born. It was not an easy decision.

I realized how unstable her life would be if she stayed with me. I am young, still growing and changing, unmarried, and was living a life in sin and chaos. I would have been unfair to bring another little one so tender – so vulnerable – into that life.

I also know the pain it causes not having a father's love and I know how it feels to feel rejected.

I cannot bear the thought of my precious baby girl suffering the same things.

Even though I love this baby with every bone in my body, I am still a kid and haven't had enough experience in handling my own life. Let alone someone in their most fragile and impressionable years to try to handle theirs.

I hope you realize, so that you can relay to her, that she is not discarded or rejected by me. That I love her so much I am willing to lose her so that she has every opportunity in life.

I went through New Beginnings because I was adamant about placing her in an Apostolic Pentecostal home. The most important thing is that this little girl's soul be saved and that she have Godly examples to pattern her life after.

I began taking care of myself by eating right, exercising, visiting the doctor and praying often. I prayed that I might get my soul right with God – and I have. And I prayed, fervently, that God would keep His hand on the little life He created and be there for her whenever she needed Him. Even when she didn't ask for His help.

My first sonogram was heart-wrenching because as I was watching her jump and wiggle inside of me, I knew she wouldn't ever be mine.

I savored every kick, punch and hiccup I felt and wondered how it would be to give up a part of me and leave it behind.

Now, after having given birth to her, I feel as if a part of my heart is dying and at times, the pain seems unbearable.

As my due date grew near, I began to have dreams in the night that would cause me to wake up crying with no one to turn to but Jesus. Many times I told Him if he didn't do something – my heart would explode.

I did have my mother and father that I could talk to. I don't know what I would've been like without them.

I went into the hospital for my scheduled C-Section, nervous and also sad. My mom was there to hold my hand as they prepared me in one of the rooms and as they wheeled me into pre-op.

In the operating room I laid for what seemed like hours and listened to the doctor banter with the nurses before I heard the startling squall of my newborn baby girl. My heart just about beat itself out of my chest and my head soared with the thought that I actually helped create this beautiful, little, miniature person.

Babies can be beautiful when they are someone else's, but when it's yours, there's nothing – and there are not any words – to describe that feeling every time you look at her.

The next three and a half days were at the same time – the happiest and the saddest days – in my life.

I watched her skin turn from a purple color to a beautiful olive – and all of her soft black hair was amazing to me.

Every facial expression, to the soft sucking sound she made when eating from the bottle was most precious. I could not touch and kiss her enough because I knew I only had a few days to be her mommy.

I both envy you and rejoice for you that you will get to see so much of her life that I'm not able to. I will continually be wondering how my little one is doing and you could put my mind at ease by sending me updates – such as when she says her first words, takes her first steps, when she receives the Holy Ghost, some funny things she says, when she gets engaged, etc... Otherwise, I will go crazy wondering.

When the day came for my baby and I to part ways, I sat in the hospital chair holding her and looking at every detail – kissing her over and over, feeling her soft hair against my face and lips.

I couldn't let her go – terrified I would forget something – the way she smelled or breathed...

I carried her out to her foster parent's vehicle in my wheelchair and placed her in the car seat so reluctant to release her. I remember looking at her for the last time. She looked so tiny and alone in this big world.

As I watched the van drive away with my heart inside, I didn't know if I could survive that moment.

That fact that she was on her way to a family who could provide her with so much more than I can right now and that God loves her and will protect her was my saving grace.

Please love this precious, tiny girl with every thing you are. And even though it won't be me – she needs a mommy and a daddy and I want her to be able to love you and know that you will never leave her side, no matter what circumstance may arise.

She also needs to know that Jesus loved her so much he died for her and whatever her need – he'll take care of.

Choosing parents was a long and sometimes difficult process. My family and I prayed and discussed, prayed and discussed and asked tons of questions. Finally, we narrowed the list down to you – and I know God had you picked out from the beginning and was there to guide us.

I hope you will tell her that her biological mother really loves her so much, but I am still working out some major problems in my life. She was not carelessly given away, but was carefully placed with a lot of prayer and a lot of pain, into a family better suited to meet her needs.

I have this terrible fear that she will be angry with me. Maybe it will help if she knows how much I love her and I realize she is not a baby doll or pet to be played with. She is a person with emotions, feelings and most important of all, a soul that must be saved.

Perhaps knowing this, she won't resent me or feel abandoned. This has been the most difficult thing in my life to do, but I want the best for her.

I believe that one day I will meet my little one again, be it in heaven, or if the Lord tarries, here on Earth. I will always love her as a mother loves her child, but I have given you the joyous responsibility to be her mommy and daddy. I would never do anything to try and deprive her of that.

I am thrilled for her that you are so excited to be able to love and kiss this little lady and be her family whom she can trust and feel secure with. I am so thankful for you and am so looking forward to the day when I will meet you and see her new brother's face.

I love you as my family and will pray for you and your new baby girl. Congratulations for the gift God has given you.

Her Birthmother

Grandparents—The "Story" Goes on Thanks to Adoption
Tom & Debbie Velie

Over twenty three years ago, Corinne Renee entered our lives.

"Everything" changed with the arrival of our beautiful six-month old baby girl from Korea.

Three years later, Shaina Lynn joined her older sister by adoption and our family was complete.

It's funny how we capture the moment we're in and think, "Things will never change."

However, in December 2003, at 3:07 p.m. our world changed with the addition of our grandson, Thomas Ethan Taylor (born 9 lbs and 5 oz. to Corinne). What a wonderful Christmas gift to all of us. This truly was a "new beginning" and we delightedly enjoyed the moment.

Through the years, hundreds of infants have spent a few days with our family while waiting for their adoptive parents to arrive.

Thomas Ethan is different; we don't have to let him go. But this experience, reminds me of how precious life really is. And for adoptive parents who wait, hoping for a baby to enter their lives soon, we pray, that they will be blessed by this book and by the entry of a child into their lives just as soon as possible.

Sometime in the not-too-distant future, a baby will be blessed with a "forever" family because others care. If you've purchased this book, you're helping us accomplish that task. On behalf the hundreds whose lives have been changed by adoption through New Beginnings, "Thank you for caring and for sharing!"

What Is Adoption?
Tom Velie

Thank you for purchasing and reading this book. Perhaps many of your questions about adoption have been answered or, perhaps, you have more questions than ever before. If there is one thing that is true about an adoption it is this, every family is different.

This book cannot begin to address the questions of cost, time on waiting lists, custody and other legal issues, termination of parental rights processes, ICPC processing, birthmother preferences specific to each adoption, open-versus-closed and everything-in-between, and the list goes on.

In general, the cost of and waiting period for an infant adoption vary based on variables related to the child and birthparent situations, including age, sex, ethnicity, geographical location of the parties, birthmother preferences, considerations for at-risk placement, and the list goes on.

Some believe adoption costs are exorbitant, but I remind them of three things:

- It cost Debbie and I, $6,500 to adopt Cori in 1982 - about the same as our new car. What does an adoption cost now in comparison to a new car?

- Thanks to our lawmakers in Washington, an adoption tax credit of over $10,000 is available.

- The waiting time allows you to save or to seek other financial options.

As the Director of a licensed, non-profit agency, I believe there are hundreds of quality adoptions agencies that are staff by good and honest people who are sacrificing better paying jobs for the sake of adoption.

Operating an agency is a costly endeavor and operating an agency with a fully-staffed maternity care center is a very costly endeavor. I know. My advice is to seek out a variety of resources, do your homework, check with licensing agencies, attorney general's offices in your state and to pray for divine guidance.

New Beginnings International Children's & Family Services is here to answer your questions and to offer professional assistance.

Final Words
Debbie Velie

I've worked New Beginnings for the past 14 years and my husband joined me there almost three years ago.

We believe in adoption on a personal level – we have two beautiful adopted Korean daughters who are now 20 and 23. Our oldest daughter is married and has blessed us with a beautiful and very busy grandson. Cori, our oldest daughter, is working to finish her degree in social work and is also on staff at New Beginnings. Our birthmothers love to talk with her – they can find out from her personal perspective how adopted children feel.

What is unique about New Beginnings as an agency is that we have the only maternity care center in the state of Mississippi. This is an expensive endeavor, but one that we have found to be vital to many of our clients through the years.

When they choose to stay at the Maternity Care Center, we know they have had consistent prenatal care, a "usually" healthy diet and counseling. We have truly been able to make a difference in the lives of many birthmothers.

Telling the Truth About Adoption

Adoption is a good thing, although you might not guess that from the perspective the media presents. When adoption makes the news, it's not typically a "happy ending" story. Sadly, this probably keeps more birthmothers from considering adoption.

And, I'm sure it also affects potential adoptive parents' feelings about adoption.

However, what the media does not tell you is that when an adoption is handled by a licensed agency, it is not like what they may see in the paper or hear on the news.

Obviously, there are risks in adoption. Our attorney stresses that to each of our adoptive couples. But, we can also assure them that if the adoption is handled by a reputable and ethical agency, the risk is drastically reduced. The highly publicized cases were not handled by licensed agencies.

Legitimate agencies do not make illegal or unethical payments to birthparents. Birthparents are offered counseling before and after the adoption. Diligent search is accomplished for birthfathers if they are not part of the process. Agency staff are trained professionals who work to protect everyone involved in the process – especially the child.

Adoptive families are screened and educated about adoption. It's not about "finding a baby," but about providing babies with stable, safe and loving homes.

What the media does not portray is that birthmothers who choose adoption are brave and unselfish. They choose adoption because they want their baby to have life and a loving, stable home. They understand that they will grieve the loss of the opportunity to parent their child. But, these brave birthmothers care more for the welfare of their child than their own feelings.

When people find out what we do, I often hear, "I don't know how someone could give their baby away." It gives me the chance to tell them, "Birthmothers don't 'give their babies away.' They made a plan for their child. They loved the baby enough to provide through the adoptive family what she could not provide herself. That is truly an unselfish and courageous decision."

Adoption is Not a Recent Concept

Adoption has existed in some form in every society throughout history. Studies have shown that throughout history, adoption was practiced by almost every human society. This is because there will always be circumstances that prevent a biological parent from caring for a child.

Adoption Practice Has Changed

Just as the practice of medicine has changed dramatically over the last few years, the practice of adoption has changed as well.

In my years at New Beginnings, I've seen many positive changes in adoption procedures.

Birthmothers are very involved in choosing the adoptive family. Many of the birthmothers we work with choose to meet the adoptive parents and although many of them choose to maintain some privacy on their part, they receive pictures and updates about the child from the adoptive parents through the agency for as long as they desire.

Every birthmother is unique and most have a very definite idea about how their adoption should work. It's very interesting when I meet with a birthmother to discover what it important to her in choosing a family.

Several years ago we worked with a client that had a long list of requirements for a family for her child. She was very specific and, thankfully, she perfectly described one of the families on our list, including the fact that they had a dog. It was a perfect match of birthmother and family and they continue to send beautiful pictures and letters to her through our office.

Not every birthmother is so involved. Some say, "I'm working with you because I trust you - you decide which family would be the best for my baby."

Then we have the other end of the spectrum – the birthmother who not only wants to choose the family and meet them, but wants a totally open adoption.

I worked with a birthmother who was older and had done a significant amount of research on open adoption. She met with me and presented her findings. After she chose a family, I called them to be sure they were willing to be as open as she was requesting. Thankfully, they were and in her words, I would like to let you know how it turned out.....

"You took my dream of a 'perfect adoption' and made it a reality. My baby will have a wonderful home life. You championed my cause and I can never thank you enough for it!"

International Adoption

International adoption has become a much more common option as well. Some families choose international adoption simply because of their fear of their adopted child being reclaimed by a birthparent. Some choose it because it can be much faster.

Our Clients

Each client we see brings her own set of strengths, challenges and problems, as well as resources and values. There is no typical client – we have worked with clients ranging in age from 12 to 44 and their reasons for making an adoption plan were unique to each of their circumstances.

However, one reason they are choosing adoption becomes clear – they do not feel that they are physically, emotionally or financially ready to parent a child at this point in their lives.

They may not have a stable home life themselves, they may want to finish school and do not believe they can do that and parent a child or they may not have the support of the birthfather or their families.

One client shared her very sad story with us. She stated that she was born to a very young birthmother who was not ready to be a parent. She related her terror of being locked in a closet while her mother went out with her friends. Although this client was in her 20's when she became pregnant, she determined that she was not ready to be a parent yet. She wanted a home for her baby where they would have security, safety and love. She chose a family, met them and decided they were perfect. She continues to stay in touch with us and is thrilled with this family and the home they have provided for her child.

When meeting with birthmothers, we always explain to them what adoptive parents must do to be approved. There is an application process that includes references and autobiographies.

After approval, families must complete a home study, which includes criminal and child abuse registry checks. We are also required to do 2 post-placement visits with the family.

Our clients are always reassured by this information.

Although an adoption plan is not for everyone, for many birthmothers, it is the best option. When you consider the large numbers of children entering the foster care system because of abuse and serious neglect and the struggles of some teen and single parents and their children, one could conclude that adoption might have been the best choice for them.

My husband and I used to work at a children's home and were house parents for 14 boys. When a child would open up and begin to share their tragic story, I often wondered how their lives would have been different if their birthparents had considered adoption.

I would like to share just a few positive adoption statistics. These statistics are encouraging for birthmothers considering adoption – they want to know their child has a chance to do well.

The following statistics are taken from published studies:

Compared with unmarried mothers who parent their children, unmarried teens who choose adoption generally:

Are more likely to finish school and obtain a higher level of education.

Attain better employment and have more financial stability.

Are less likely to repeat or abort another unplanned pregnancy.

Are more likely to marry in the future and when they do, are more likely to delay marriage to an older age.

Report a high level of satisfaction with their adoption decision.

In contrast, teens who choose to parent their children face a large number of challenges from social, financial and emotional perspectives:

Are more likely to repeat an out-of-wedlock pregnancy.

Are more likely to remain unmarried and to have children who experience out-of-wedlock pregnancy.

Are more likely to have serious employment and financial problems.

Only 20% of unmarried mothers receive child support from the child's father.

Another study revealed a sobering statistic:

Over 70% of juveniles in state reform institutions are from fatherless homes. The lack of a father is more important than any other factor, including income, for predicting criminal behavior.

A *Search Institute Study* is the largest to date on adoption and reflects the same outcomes as other major adoption studies.

Specifically they found:

Adoptive parents are less likely to be divorced and more likely to have college degrees.

Adopted children are less likely to live with a single parent.

Adopted adolescents scored higher on indicators of well-being such as: school performance, friendships, volunteerism, optimism, self-esteem, social competency, feelings of support from others and low level of anxiety.

Adopted adolescents scored lower on indicators of high risk behaviors such as: use of alcohol, depression, vandalism, group fighting, police trouble, theft, weapon use, driving/riding while drinking and seat belt non-use.

Children adopted trans-racially showed no differences in terms of identity formation and self-esteem, attachment to parents or psychological health.

There is a common misconception that adoption in the past harmed children and birthparents because of the lack of contact between them in confidential adoptions. The studies we just looked at show that children in this era have fared well and feel secure in their adoptive families. Only now is data beginning to appear on the outcomes of children adopted after 1980 with a new "open" approach.

As Mississippi law stands today, if an adopted person wishes to search for a birth parent, they must be at least 21 and they must receive birthparent search counseling from a licensed agency.

Our agency is fairly young and none of our babies are old enough to search at this point, but we do the birthparent search counseling for adoptees.

These sessions have been very rewarding and reassuring for me. Since adoption work is what I do and believe in, it has been rewarding to meet with adults who were adopted and to have them express their thankfulness to their birthparents for choosing adoption.

During the counseling, we have to explore their relationship with their adoptive parents and why they are searching. In every case, they tell me that they want their birthparent to know they are okay and to say thank you.

We also assist in coordinating adoptions for out-of-state agencies.

While we were in the room with one of the birthmothers and the adoptive family, a nurse came into the room and asked if she could say something to the birthmother. She shared that she had placed a baby for adoption 30 years earlier. She said that very few people knew she had made that plan. She stated that the agency contacted her a few weeks earlier and told her that her son would like to meet her.

She said, "When I walked into the room to meet him, my first words were, 'I'm sorry.'"

He said, "You have no nothing to be sorry about. You made a decision that was the best for both of us at the time. I have had a wonderful life and I have wonderful parents and I want to tell you 'Thank you.'"

We worked with an older birthmom several years ago. When she met the adoptive parents, her one main concern was that the child would someday be "mad" at her for making this decision. The adoptive father leaned forward in his chair and said to her, "You will be his hero."

One younger adopted child put it this way, "If I could talk to my birthmom, I'd tell her I'm glad that she brought me to my parents. When I told this to people in my class, they were shocked. I guess they just don't understand that I think I have the best life anybody could have."

Parenting a child is a commitment to provide a stable, loving and permanent environment for a child.

An adoption decision does not involve "keeping" or "giving away" a baby. It actually involves a choice for parenting or choosing an adoptive family to parent the child.

The decision to not parent, when accompanied by an adoption plan, is NOT abandonment.

Some birthmothers may experience a sense of guilt when making this decision until they realize that when they choose adoption, they are not "abandoning" the child, they are assuring that the child **will** have a stable home with a couple who is ready to parent.

An adoption choice is a life transition that can be difficult and emotional; it is not a lifelong grieving and recovery process.

When we are counseling with birthmothers, we discuss the grieving process that they can expect to experience. We also let them know that they will never forget that child, but that time is healing, just as it is with any event in our lives that causes grief.

A *Battelle Research study* that compared teens who made an adoption plan with teens who chose to parent, shows the same high level of satisfaction with their decisions.

We also stress to our birthmoms that they may stay in touch with us for as long as they need to. They call to let us know they are doing well or that they have married.

One birthmother wrote it this way:

"Remember, a woman can heal from this. It is not a lifelong process. It is a fact that she is a birthmother and she can find great peace and comfort in her unselfish act of love. However, it does not have to consume the rest of her life. She can allow the experience to transform her. When I received the most recent letter and pictures from my daughter's adoptive parents, I realized that I had finished my grieving process. As I looked at the beautiful pictures, I thought to myself, 'What a beautiful child; but, she is not mine.' Although forever my firstborn, she is not my family now, nor am I hers. A job well done."

Communication about adoption is done with relative ease and comfort according to a 1994 study. This study revealed that teens stated that they had two or fewer conversations about adoption with either parent in the past year. Yet, most feel comfortable talking with their parents about adoption issues.

We encourage our adoptive parents to normalize adoption from the very beginning. The days are gone when adoptive parents pretend that they gave birth to the child and keep the adoption a secret. When we do a home study, that is an issue that is discussed.

In our case, it was very obvious and we were amazed at how young Cori was when she realized she did not look like us. We were in a restaurant and she noticed an Asian couple a few booths over. She said, "Look, there's like Cori."

But for other families, where the children may resemble them in looks, most choose to do a photo album that begins the day they meet the birthmother or come to the hospital. They usually include photos at the agency and ones taken with the judge when we go to court. It gives the child a history of how he came to belong to his family.

Accurate Adoption Language

There has been a lot of emphasis in the adoption field about positive adoption language.

Because, words not only convey facts, they also evoke feelings. For example, when the news details a "custody battle" between the "real" parents and the "other" parents, it reinforces the inaccurate notion that only birthparents are real parents and that adoptive parents are not real parents. And potential adoptive parents may wrongly conclude that all adoptions end in "battles."

Accurate language can help to stop the spread of misconceptions such as these.

Inaccurate Language	Accurate Language
Real or Natural Parent	Birthparent
Own child, real child, natural child	Birthchild
Adopted child	My child
Giving up or giving away your child	Making an adoption plan
Putting your child up for adoption	Finding a family to parent
Keeping your baby	Deciding to parent the child
Foreign adoption	International Adoption

Examining and correcting adoption language is just the start. Sadly, the field of adoption has been negatively affected by the media.

Part of our job as adoption professionals is to help spread the word that adoption can be a very good thing.

Put simply, the definition of adoption is this --

"Adoption is a means of providing caring and responsible parents for children who need them."

Adoption is about and for children

Although the birthparents are the only ones who can make the adoption plan – they are doing so because they believe it is the best for the baby. When we work with birthmothers, I remind them that they are also speaking for the person in the equation that cannot speak for itself – the child.

One birthmother put it this way:

"I knew that my decision would be the hardest thing in the world for me. But it wasn't about me. It was about her. It was about what I could give her: a family, stability and a chance for the future."

ADOPTION DEFINITIONS

Confidential Adoption: An adoption where only non-identifying social and medical information is exchanged between parties to an adoption through the agency.

141

As we discussed before, not every birthmother is interested in an open adoption. However, as a licensed agency, we are required to disclose all available information regarding medical and social information about the birthparents with the adoptive parents.

Semi-open adoption: Used to describe a range of practices that involves the exchange of information and contact between birth parents and adoptive parents. It usually includes using first names and exchanging information and letters and pictures through the agency.

Open Adoption: An adoption where identifying information has been exchanged between the birthparents and the adoptive parents and they have established direct, ongoing contact.

Trans-racial Adoption: An adoption in which a child of one race is adopted by a parent or parents of another race.
And finally, **adoption is not foster care**. Foster care is and should be – temporary. Adoption is permanent and stable.

In my personal experience, adoption has been an awesome way for me to be a parent. I can't imagine that I could love my daughters any more if they had been born to me.

I have a friend that runs an adoption agency in another city. She says, *"I don't think it's that adoptive parents love their children more that the rest of us, but I do think they appreciate them more."*

One adoptive parent put it this way, *"A family is a family. It doesn't matter how it comes to us."*

Thank you for considering adoption!

142

In Closing, A Special Memorial Tribute
Tom & Debbie Velie

Our attempt at a *Thank You* page ended with the use of the "CTRL-A and DELETE" functions on the computer.

There were simply too many people to thank and we knew that someone would be unintentionally left out. Everyone, including family and friends, have been supportive of the adoption process in our family and in our life's work. So, as we close this first edition of stories, we extend our heartfelt appreciation to everyone who supports adoption.

However, our story would not be complete without offering a special tribute to Aunt Marilyn Jensen, who went home to be with the Lord in September 1999. Marilyn loved children and we always looked forward to visiting Marilyn and her husband, Gordon.

She always had an itinerary prepared before we arrived—the zoo, the park, the museum, cupcakes in the yard and games in the evening. Marilyn loved people...especially children. Every child needs an "Aunt Marilyn."

Marilyn and Gordon played the role of *Stork* for our family. In both 1982 and 1985, they traveled to pick up Cori and Shaina and bring them "home" to us.

Gordon was a lifelong employee of Northwest Airlines so the girls received special treatment on the flights. You knew this because they were the last to disembark from the giant 747's. It wasn't just being the last one off the plane, it was the fact that half of the plane's occupants would line the path in the terminal as they delivered our daughters to us.

Even though we lived a thousand miles apart from Marilyn and Gordon, we knew that we would be welcome to visit any time - especially if we had Cori and Shaina with us.

Today, we can only imagine how much fun Marilyn would be having with little Ethan, our grandson. And so…thank you Marilyn for loving us, playing with us, making cupcakes for us and for teaching us the most important lesson in life.

And by the way, we know why the Lord "took you early in life." He wanted you to help arrange some of the field trips and cupcake parties in heaven.

"Children are God's special gift to all of us and we must be there - FOR THEM TO TOUCH WHEN THEY REACH OUT."

References and Resources

Links

www.adoptioncouncil.org - Great resource to identify quality adoption programs

www.newbeginnings.us – New Beginnings – our adoption agency.

www.shaohannahshope.org – Adoption grants may be available through this site

Books

Brodzinsky, Anne B., & Stanley, Diana L. (1996). *The Mulberry Bird*. Indianapolis, IN: Perspectives Press.

Keck, Gregory C., & Kupecky, Regina M. (1995). *Adopting the Hurt Child: Hope for Families with Special-Needs Kids*. Colorado Springs, CO: Pinon Press.

Keck, Gregory C., & Kupecky, Regina M. (2002). *Parenting the Hurt Child: Helping Adoptive Families Heal and Grow*. Colorado Springs, CO: Pinon Press.

Keefer, Betsy, & Schooler, Jayne E. (2000). Telling the *Truth to your Adopted or Foster Child: Making Sense of the Past*. Westport, CT: Bergin and Garvey.

Koenig, Mary A., & Berg, Niki (2000). *Sacred Connections: Stories of Adoption*. Philadelphia, PA: Running Press Book Publishers.

145

Marshner, Connaught, & Pierce, William L. (Eds.). (1999). *Adoption Factbook III*. Waite Park, MN: Park Press Quality Printing, Inc.

Schooler, Jayne E., & Norris, Betsy L. (2002). *Journeys After Adoption: Understanding Lifelong Issues*. Westport, CT: Bergin and Garvey.

Simon, Rita J., & Altstein (1987). *Trans-racial Adoptees and their Families: A Study of Identity and Commitment*. New York, NY: Prager Publishers.